Book 5
Teacher's Guide and Answer Key

VOCABULARY
FROM
CLASSICAL
ROOTS

▼ Lee Mountain ▼

EDUCATORS PUBLISHING SERVICE
Cambridge and Toronto

Cover photo credit: Erich Lessing/Art Resource, NY
Acquisitions/Development: Sethany Rancier Alongi
Editor: Mary Troeger
Senior Editorial Manager: Sheila Neylon
Typesetter: Sarah Cole

Printed in U.S.A.

ISBN 0-8388-2250-9

978-0-8388-2250-0

9 10 11 PPG 16

CONTENTS

INTRODUCTION

This teacher's guide for *Vocabulary from Classical Roots 5* complements, extends, and enriches the lessons of the student book in three ways.

First, the lesson plans help students to access prior knowledge, thereby enabling them to make connections between familiar words and new words that share the same classical root. For example, the familiar word *aquarium*, with its root *aqua*, can provide scaffolding for learning the related word *aquatic.*

Second, the lesson plans provide a variety of *oral* activities as well as additional written activities on reproducible worksheets. Discussions and games (classroom contests, synonym tic-tac-toe, charades, word puzzles, syllable sorts) lead students to incorporate the new words into their oral and written vocabularies.

Third, the lesson plans expand students' understanding of *classical roots*, the unique focus of this series. They provide teachers with a sensible and effective way to teach vocabulary from a roots-based perspective, even when a background in classical-language roots is not a part of the teacher's own experience. A knowledge of Latin and Greek roots can give students a head start on unlocking the meanings of innumerable words they will meet in the intermediate and secondary grades.

LESSON PLAN FORMAT

The lesson plans in this guide for all lessons (except review lessons) have the following headings.

Introduce Lesson

Before your students pick up their pencils, *talk* with them about the lesson title and the two featured roots or affixes.

Preview Familiar Words

Through *oral* activities, show students how the featured roots relate to the meanings of the familiar words.

Present Key Words

Build *oral* familiarity with the key words. Then have students read the words, underline the featured roots, use root clues to help with meanings, and study the full definitions.

Guide Oral Practice

Give students opportunities to use the words *orally* in two activities: "Connections and Examples" and "Draw, Display, Discuss."

Assign Written Exercises

Have students match synonyms and antonyms, fill in key words in context, and work with related roots and affixes.

Answer keys are provided for all exercises.

A reproducible worksheet for additional reinforcement is also provided for each lesson (except the review lessons). The worksheets are located at the end of the guide (see pages 63–74).

The lesson plans for all of the review lessons in this guide have these headings:

Discuss

Use oral activities for revisiting the vocabulary from the preceding three lessons.

Reinforce

Use oral activities for further practice with the material presented in each Exercise C.

Explore

Use additional word-learning strategies to review specific words (see pages vi–viii).

Guide Oral Practice

Organize classroom games such as Definition Challenge and Charades.

Assign Written Exercises

Reinforce vocabulary with activities that expand associations with words, roots, and affixes.

Answer keys are provided for the exercises.

SELECTION CRITERIA: WHY THESE WORDS AND ROOTS?

For any vocabulary textbook, the initial questions are: *which* words and *why* these words?

For answers, look at the title of this book, *Vocabulary from **Classical Roots** 5*. All the featured words are derived from classical roots. Knowing even a limited number of Latin and Greek roots can provide clues to the meanings of an unlimited number of multisyllabic words.

The next questions for this book have to be: which roots and why these roots? For answers, look at the selection criteria for deciding which roots, prefixes, and suffixes to include: frequency, usefulness, and research.

Frequency

Roots and affixes that appear on lists of the 3000 most frequently used words were chosen. These parts of words recur often in vocabulary across the curriculum.

Usefulness

From the secondary books of the *Vocabulary from Classical Roots* series, it was easy to ascertain which roots and affixes were expected to be known from the intermediate grades. These meaningful parts are featured in the books for grades 5 and 6, along with some roots that were presented at an advanced level, but are useful to intermediate students when given a simpler presentation.

Research

Publications by vocabulary authorities provided research findings as well as expert opinions on the roots and affixes that could best help intermediate students figure out word meanings. Also, the research underlying student dictionaries was helpful in determining which roots, prefixes, suffixes, and definitions were most suitable for the intermediate grades.

Now that you know the why behind the selection of words and roots in this book, let's return to the initial questions:

Which words? See the list on the last page of this book.

Which roots? See the inside front cover.

ADDITIONAL WORD-LEARNING STRATEGIES

The following word-learning strategies can be adapted for individual, small group, or whole class instruction. They are helpful in focusing attention on a particular prefix, root, or word. As students expand their word webs, fill in their Venn diagrams, and answer questions for their definition maps, they are deepening their understanding of the new words in their vocabularies.

WEBS WITH ROOTS AND AFFIXES

A root or affix web can help students identify the meaning common to a group of words. Display the root or affix in the middle of the web and discuss its meaning. Complete the web with words that contain the root or affix. Students can include different forms of the same word. Discuss definitions and relationships of the words to the root or affix.

The graphic can be as simple as the following web with *circ*, showing just a few words connected to the root or as complex as the web with *trans-*, featuring groups of related words.

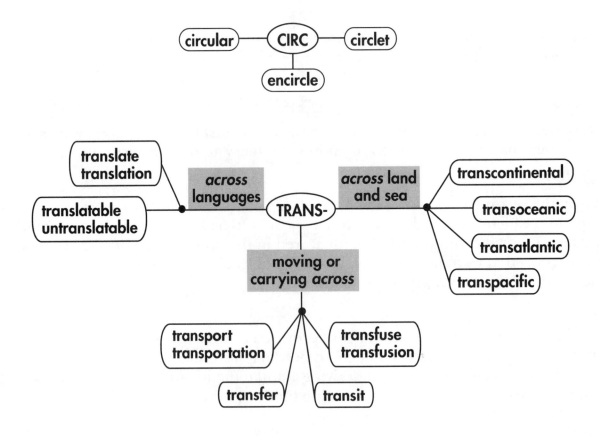

VENN DIAGRAMS

The overlapping circles of a Venn diagram can show how two words are similar and different. In the first Venn diagram below, the differences between *diameter* and *perimeter* are listed in the outer parts of the circles. The similarities are listed in the overlapping section in the middle.

In the second Venn diagram, the same procedure is followed for the words *telescope* and *telegraph*.

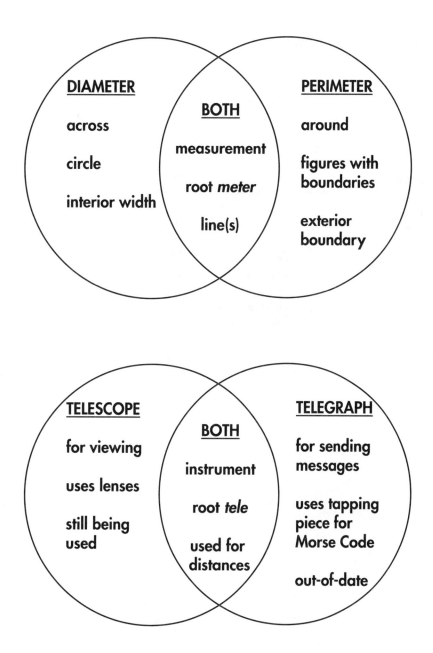

DEFINITION MAP

A definition map is a visual display that shows the common components of a dictionary definition by answering these questions about a word:

What is it?

What is it like?

What are some specific examples of the word?

What are some specific non-examples of the word?

Independently or in groups, students can fill in the map and then use the information to write an expanded definition of the word, based on the map.

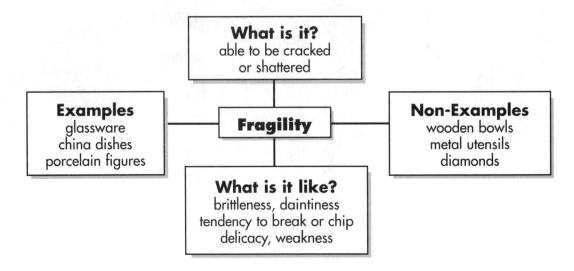

Students then use the map to write a definition for the word. For example: Fragility is the property of certain materials (such as glass, china, and porcelain) to crack, chip, break, or shatter easily.

LESSON 1: GOING IN CIRCLES (PAGES 1–4)

> ## Key Words
>
> | | | | |
> |---|---|---|---|
> | circuit | circulate | cyclone | semicircle |
> | circular | cycle | recycle | unicycle |

INTRODUCE LESSON 1

(page 1) Introduce Lesson 1 orally by having students read the title "Going in Circles" and the two featured roots *circ*, meaning "around," and *cycl*, meaning "revolving."

Ask them to think of examples of "revolving around" and "going in circles" and then to demonstrate some of these to the class. (Examples: the planets revolving around the sun, running around a track, spinning a top or a coin, tracing the circumference of a coin, rolling a ball, and so on)

PREVIEW FAMILIAR WORDS

(pages 1, 2) *circle, circus, bicycle, cyclist, motorcycle, tricycle*

Activity 1: *circ*

Display the familiar words *circle* and *circus*. Read them orally and then chorally with the class. Underline the root *circ* in each one.

Ask students the following questions:

Name some things that are round like a circle. (hoop, ring, wheel, disk)

What athletes have you seen move in circles? (Examples: a gymnast holding onto a bar and swinging her body around in a complete circle in the air, a roller skater gliding around a rink, an ice skater spinning around in one spot, and so on)

Where do circus performers do their acts? (They perform in a ring.)

Why do you think circuses are usually set up in rings? (The Circus Maximus in Rome was in a circle. Circular seating *around* the ring may allow the most people to be seated with the best view.)

Ask: What is the shared meaning for the root *circ* in the words *circle* and *circus*? (around)

Activity 2: *cycl*

Display the familiar words *bicycle, cyclist, motorcycle,* and *tricycle*. Read them orally and then chorally with the class. Underline the root *cycl* in each one.

Ask students the following questions:

Bicycles, tricycles, and motorcycles have wheels. What is the shape of the wheels? (round)

In order for these vehicles to move, what must the wheels do? (go around)

When we speak of the earth "going around" the sun, what word do we use for "going around"? (*revolving*)

Can we use that same word, *revolving*, for the turning of the wheels on a bicycle, tricycle, or motorcycle? (yes)

Which of the familiar words names a person who pedals a bicycle to make the wheels *revolve?* (*cyclist*)

Ask: What is the shared meaning for the root *cycl* in *bicycle, cyclist, motorcycle,* and *tricycle?* (revolving)

PRESENT KEY WORDS

Display the key words. Read them orally and then chorally with the class.

Have students underline the root in each key word in the box on page 1; then have them check to be sure that their words look like this.

<u>circ</u>uit	<u>circ</u>ulate	<u>cycl</u>one	semi<u>circ</u>le
<u>circ</u>ular	<u>cycl</u>e	re<u>cycl</u>e	uni<u>cycl</u>e

Ask students the following questions:

Which words begin with a root? (*circuit, circular, circulate, cycle, cyclone*)

In which words is the root not at the beginning? (*recycle, semicircle, unicycle*)

The words *recycle, semicircle,* and *unicycle* start with the prefixes *re-, semi-,* and *uni-*. You will meet *semi-* and *re-* later. But in Exercise C of this lesson, you will find out more about the prefix *uni-*. For now, can you predict the meaning of *uni-* as in *unicycle?* (one)

As students complete the "Using Root Clues" section, encourage them to use the meanings of the roots to find the correct answer. Have them match the columns <u>before</u> they study the complete definitions of the words.

Dictate the answers so that students can check themselves.

(page 1) 1. B 2. A 3. D 4. C

Present each key word, paying attention to pronunciation, part of speech, definition with context sentence, and other parts of the listing as applicable (additional derivation, related word form, illustration).

In this first lesson, take time to introduce students to the respellings that help with pronunciation.

Ask: On page 2, what letters do you see in the parentheses following the word *cyclone?*

(the letters *s i k l o n*) What is the purpose of this respelling of *cyclone*? (to show how the word is pronounced)

How many syllables do you hear in *cyclone*? (two) Which syllable is accented, or said more loudly? (the first syllable) In the respelling, where do you see the accent mark? (after the first syllable, to show that it is the accented syllable)

In the respelling, what do you see over each vowel? (a line, or long mark, called a macron)

Turn back to the inside front cover, and look at the "Key to Diacritical Marks."

Which four vowels have long marks over them? (*a, e, i,* and *o*)

Look at the first letter of the key word that follows each vowel—*apron, even, ivy,* and *open.* In each case, what do you notice about the sound of the initial letter? (It is the same as the name of the letter.) What is the respelling of the long sound of *u*? (the letter *y* followed by the two-dot *u*)

What other vowel is shown with two dots over it? (*a*) What is the sound of the two-dot *a*? (ah, as in *father*)

What is the sound of the symbol that looks like an upside down *e*? (uh, as in *around*) What is the name of that symbol? (schwa)

Look again at the respelling of *cyclone* on page 2. If you had no previous acquaintance with the word *cyclone*, would the respelling with diacritical marks enable you to pronounce it correctly? (yes)

GUIDE ORAL PRACTICE

Activity 1: Connections and Examples

Explain that sometimes there is a strong literal connection between the meaning of a word and the meaning of its root. The connection is very easy to see. Other times the connection is not as literal, so it is not as easy to see.

Which word—*cyclone* or *recycle*—has the more literal connection with the "revolving" meaning of *cycl*? (*Cyclone* has the more literal connection because in a cyclone, or tornado or hurricane or twister, you can actually see the revolving motion of the material that the wind is whirling around. To *recycle* is to fix something for another round of use, but its connection with the "revolving, turning, spinning" meanings of *cycl* is not as literal.)

The root *circ* makes people think of a circle, and therefore of roundness. Which word—*circular* or *circulate*—has a stronger connection with the idea of roundness? (*Circular,* since it describes the shape of a circle. To *circulate* is to move around, but not necessarily in a circle.)

Activity 2: Draw, Display, Discuss

Ask: Which of the eight featured words is easiest to draw? (a semicircle)

Have students draw and display semicircles. Discuss differences between their drawings, and the difficulties of freehand drawing of a semicircle. Ask students how they can make a perfect circle. (by using a compass, a piece of string tied to a pencil and rotated around a fixed point, a template such as a lid). Using one of these methods, have students draw a circle and then a line through its middle to make two semicircles.

Ask: Which other words could you show in a drawing? (probably *unicycle* and *cyclone*, maybe *circuit*, from diagrams in science textbooks. If students try to draw circular *things*, point out that the word *circular* is an adjective that describes those things.)

Where have you seen a unicycle? (at a street fair, at a circus)

Where and when have you seen a cyclone? (Some students may have had personal experiences with windstorms or may have seen some on television or in a movie.)

What happens when a circuit breaker shuts off? (The electricity cannot get through.)

Why does a circuit breaker shut down? (More electricity is going through the wire than the wire can carry without catching on fire.)

The report card cycle rolls around time and time again. What is the report card cycle at our school? (Answers will vary: monthly, six weeks, and so on.)

ASSIGN WRITTEN EXERCISES

Exercise A: Synonyms (page 3)

1. c   2. a   3. d   4. d   5. c

Exercise B: Meaning in Context (page 3)

1. unicycle   2. circular   3. semicircle   4. circulate   5. cyclone

Exercise C: Extend Your Vocabulary (page 4)

(Sentences will vary for 1–5, but sample sentences are provided.)

1. triangle 3: A triangle is a figure with three sides and three angles.

2. united 1: United means joined into one; being in agreement.

3. bilingual 2: Bilingual means able to speak two languages.

4. unicorn 1: A unicorn is a mythical creature that looks like a white horse with one horn.

5. triplet 3: Triplets are three of a kind, such as three babies born of the same mother at the same time.

Reproducible Worksheet: Lesson 1 (page 63 in this book)

LESSON 2: BALANCING EVENLY (PAGES 5–8)

> ## Key Words
>
> | dependent | equate | equidistant | pending |
> |-----------|--------|-------------|---------|
> | equality | equator | equilateral | pendulum |

INTRODUCE LESSON 2

(page 5) Introduce Lesson 2 orally by having students read the title "Balancing Evenly" and the two featured roots *equ*, meaning "same, even, equal," and *pend*, meaning "hanging; weighing in the balance."

Students may have seen statues or images on television representing "Justice" as a blindfolded goddess holding something aloft. See if they know what the "something" is. (It is a balance scale with plates for weights hanging from both sides. When the weights hanging on both sides of the scale are equal, the scale of justice is evenly balanced.)

PREVIEW FAMILIAR WORDS

(pages 5, 6) *equal, equally, equivalent, unequal, depend, dependable, suspenders*

Activity 1: *equ*

Display the familiar words *equal, equally, equivalent, unequal*. Read them orally and then chorally with the class. Underline the root *equ* in each one.

Ask students the following questions:

In which subject have you met these words? (math)

What is the symbol for the word *equal*? (=)

Which of the familiar words means "not equal"? (*unequal*)

What part of that word carries the "not" meaning? (the prefix *un-*)

Draw a rectangle on the board. Have a student draw an equivalent figure. Then ask the class if these figures are the *same*. (yes)

Write this sentence on the board: The two cups of cocoa are _____ sweet.

Suppose you added a teaspoon of sugar to each of these two cups of cocoa. Use one of the familiar words to complete the sentence. (*equally*)

Ask: What are the shared meanings for the root *equ* in the words *equal, equally, equivalent, unequal*? (same, equal)

Activity 2: *pend*

Display the familiar words *depend, dependable, suspenders.* Read them orally and then chorally with the class. Underline the root *pend* in each one.

Ask students the following questions:

What is the purpose of suspenders? (They hold up pants.)

How do suspenders work? (They have three points of attachment, two at the front of the pants and one at the back. These hold up the pants evenly.)

Mountain climbers *depend* on their ropes. To climb safely, they must have *dependable* ropes that they can *hang* on to. What root do the words *depend* and *dependable* share? (*pend*)

What is the meaning of that root? (hanging)

What is a dependable person like? (Such a person is one you can count on or rely on.)

How are a dependable person and the mountain climbers' ropes alike? (You can be sure of your safety as you *hang* onto, or rely on, them.)

Ask: What is the shared meaning for the root *pend* in *depend, dependable, suspenders?* (hanging)

PRESENT KEY WORDS

Display the key words. Read them orally and then chorally with the class.

Have students underline the root in each key word in the box on page 5; then have them check to be sure that their words look like this.

de<u>pend</u>ent	<u>equ</u>ate	<u>equ</u>idistant	<u>pend</u>ing
<u>equ</u>ality	<u>equ</u>ator	<u>equ</u>ilateral	<u>pend</u>ulum

Only one of the eight featured words does *not* begin with a root. Which one? (*dependent*)

The adjective *dependent* is often used to describe people. When have you been completely dependent on others? (as a baby, during an illness, while recovering from an accident)

As people grow up, they become more independent. What does *independent* mean? (not relying on others, not dependent) What do you call the words *dependent* and *independent?* (antonyms, because they are opposites)

As students complete the "Using Root Clues" section, encourage them to use the meanings of the roots to find the correct answer. Have them match the columns <u>before</u> they study the complete definitions of the words.

Dictate the answers so that students can check themselves.

(page 5) 1. C   2. D   3. B   4. A

Present each key word, paying attention to pronunciation, part of speech, definition with context sentence, and other parts of the listing as applicable (additional derivation, related word form, illustration).

In this lesson, pay particular attention to the related word form. The listings in this book include many related words that are formed by adding the noun suffix *-ion* to the key word, as in *equate/equation*.

Say: On page 6, at the top of the page, read the complete listing for the verb *equate*. On the very last line of that listing, what related word do you see? (*equation*) What does the "n." after the related form *equation* mean? (It means that *equation* is a noun.)

Is the noun *equation* more familiar to you than the verb *equate*? (probably, because it appears so often in math books) If you know the definition of *equation*, what information does that give you about the definition of *equate*? (It tells you *equate* is connected to the idea of *equal*.) Use the two words in a sentence. (Example: You *equate* the numbers on the two sides of the equal sign to make an *equation*.)

Turn back to page 2, and find a key word that is a verb which has a related form that is a noun. (*circulate/circulation*) Use these two words in a sentence. (Example: When we studied the human body's system of *circulation*, we learned that blood *circulates* through veins and arteries.)

GUIDE ORAL PRACTICE

Activity 1: Connections and Examples

Sometimes there is a very strong connection between the meaning of a word and the meaning of its root. Other times the connection is not so strong.

Which word—*equality* or *equator*—has a stronger connection with the "equal" meaning of *equ*? (*Equality* has a stronger connection, because the definition of equality is "the condition of being <u>equal</u>." The "equal connection" for *equator* is the fact that this imaginary line is *equidistant* from the North Pole and the South Pole, definitely a connection with <u>equal</u>, but not as strong a connection.)

Have a student point out the *equator* on a classroom map or globe. Ask: What is the climate of equatorial countries? (hot)

Can anyone explain why? (The position of the midsection of the earth in relation to the sun experiences the least amount of change as the earth rotates around the sun. This is because of the angle of the earth's axis.)

Which word—*pendulum* or *pending*—has a more literal connection with the "hanging" meaning of the root *pend*? (*Pendulum* because it is an object you can actually see hanging from a clock. You can't see an actual image for the word *pending*, but you can imagine the situation of a committee trying to reach a decision. Until they agree, their decision is *pending*, hanging, not yet determined.)

Activity 2: Draw, Display, Discuss

Ask: Which of the featured words is easiest to draw? (probably *pendulum*)

Has anyone seen a clock with a pendulum? Describe it. (Answers will vary, since some students may have clocks with pendulums at home and other may have seen them in stores or on television.)

Display two unequal pieces of chalk. How can you *equate*, or make equal, the lengths of these two chalk pieces? (They can be broken to be the same.)

Put out a selection of coins and bills of different value, such as pennies, nickels, dimes, quarters, and a dollar bill. Ask different students to make combinations that *equate*. (four quarters and a dollar, five pennies and a nickel, and so on)

On a piece of notebook paper, ask students to quickly draw triangles and then hold them up for viewing. Ask: Which triangle comes closest to being *equilateral*, that is, having three sides of the same length?

Which desk in our classroom is *equidistant* from the two side walls?

Draw a large circle on the board. Ask a student to draw a diameter. Ask: What point in a circle is equidistant from the two ends of the diameter? (the center of the circle)

ASSIGN WRITTEN EXERCISES

Exercise A: Synonyms (page 7)

1. a   2. b   3. d   4. a   5. c

Exercise B: Meaning in Context (page 7)

1. equidistant   2. pendulum   3. equator   4. depending

Exercise C: Extend Your Vocabulary (page 8)

1. C   2. 4   3. 4   4. 4   5. 4

Reproducible Worksheet: Lesson 2 (page 64 in this book)

LESSON 3: MOVING ACROSS AND BETWEEN (PAGES 9–12)

Key Words

interactive	intersect	transfer
interfere	interval	transfusion
intermittent	transact	transmit

INTRODUCE LESSON 3

(page 9) Introduce Lesson 3 orally by having the students read the title "Moving Across and Between" and the two featured prefixes *trans-*, meaning "across," and *inter-*, meaning "between."

Point out that sometimes these prefixes share meanings. Consider the word *Internet.* Messages and information travel *across* distances and *between* people on the Internet. Consider the word *transatlantic.* A transatlantic flight is *across* the ocean and *between* two continents. Meanings connected with *across* and *between* sometimes overlap.

PREVIEW FAMILIAR WORDS

(pages 9, 10) *transform, transparent, transplant, transportation, intermediate, interstate*

Activity 1: *trans-*

Display the familiar words *transform, transparent, transplant, transportation.* Read them orally and then chorally with the class. Underline the prefix *trans-* in each one.

Ask students the following questions:

Which word could be used to describe moving a plant from one location *across* a yard to another location? (*transplant*)

What forms of transportation are available in our community? (car, bus, taxi, bicycle, plane, truck, horse, and so on)

From outside, could you see into a room if its curtains were *transparent?* (Yes, and note that *across* can carry the meaning "through," since see-through curtains allow your vision to pass *across* from one side of the curtain to the other side.)

Ask students to transform the expression on their face by showing different emotions. What emotions are they showing and what is happening to their face as they make the changes? (The appearance of their face changes as they show different emotions.)

Ask: What is the shared meaning for the prefix *trans-* in the words *transform, transparent, transplant, transportation?* (across)

Activity 2: *inter-*

Display the familiar words *intermediate* and *interstate*. Read them orally and then chorally with the class. Underline *inter-* in each one.

Ask students the following questions:

In our school district, what grades are considered *intermediate*? (Answers will probably range from 4–6 to 4–8.)

Why are they called intermediate? (because they come *between* the primary grades and the secondary grades)

Distribute several road maps or road atlases to groups of students. Ask them to look at the map legend, or key, to see the different colors and symbols used to mark roads. Ask: What interstate highways cross our state? How are these marked on the map? (Have a student draw the symbol on the board. This may or may not include the word *interstate*.)

Where do the interstate highways go when they leave our state? (to the bordering states)

Do the interstate highways cross the border *between* our state and other states? (yes)

Ask: What is the shared meaning for the prefix *inter-* in *intermediate* and *interstate*? (between)

PRESENT KEY WORDS

Display the key words. Read them orally and then chorally with the class.

Have students underline the prefix in each key word in the box on page 9; then have them check to be sure that their words look like this.

interactive	intermittent	interval	transfer	transmit
interfere	intersect	transact	transfusion	

There are nine key words in Lesson 3. How many begin with a prefix? (all nine)

The roots, as well as the prefixes, of some of the key words can give you clues to meaning.

Are you familiar with other forms of any of the words on the list? Write the words the students identify on the board and ask them to explain their meanings. (For example, *interference*, *intersection*, car *transmission*, and so on)

As students complete the "Using Prefix Clues" section, encourage them to use the meanings of the prefixes to find the correct answer. Have them match the columns <u>before</u> they study the complete definitions of the words.

Dictate the answers so that students can check themselves.

(page 9) 1. C 2. A 3. D 4. B

Present each key word, paying attention to pronunciation, part of speech, definition with context sentence, and other parts of the listing as applicable (additional derivation, related word form, illustration).

In this lesson, pay particular attention to additional derivations.

Ask: On page 10, which three words have information inside brackets [ ] following the respellings? (2. transfer, 3. transfusion, and 6. interfere) What kind of information is given inside the brackets? (information about the other Latin roots that appear in the words)

In the case of *transfer*, what does *trans-* mean? (across) The other part of the word, *fer*, is derived from the Latin word *ferre*, meaning "to carry." When you put together the two parts, what meaning do you have for *transfer*, based strictly on derivations from Latin? (to carry across)

Why is the other derivation especially meaningful in the case of *transfusion?* (The connection with "to pour" is especially applicable to blood transfusions.)

For *interfere*, the connection with "to strike" is not quite as strong. But in sports, what can "running interference" mean? (pushing others out of the way, maybe even striking them down)

If a word has both a prefix and a root derived from Latin or Greek, how many clues do you have toward its meaning? (two)

GUIDE ORAL PRACTICE

Activity 1: Connections and Examples

Point to the word *interval*. Say: An interval is "a time between." What are some examples of intervals? (Examples: Summer is the interval between the ending and the starting of the school year. November to January is the interval between electing and inaugurating the president. There are intervals between races at a track meet, and between quarters and halves of other athletic events.)

Demonstrate *intermittent* buzzing: Bzzz … silence … bzzz … silence … bzzz … Have students give other examples of intermittent sounds. (some kinds of alarms, knocking on a door, dripping of a leaky faucet)

Activity 2: Draw, Display, Discuss

Ask students to draw two streets near the school or near their homes that intersect. Ask: Have there been many accidents there? (Answers will vary.)

What makes intersections dangerous? (There can be more cars because traffic from two different streets are crossing each other. Drivers or pedestrians don't obey the signals.)

Buying a bus ticket is a business *transaction* since you pay for the ticket. Do you pay again for a transfer? (No, you don't because a transfer gives you free access from one bus to another to complete your ride.) What are other forms of transportation that might provide a transfer? (some trains and subways)

What keys on the keyboard of a computer (or directions on the monitor) do you use most often to *transmit* material? (enter, send)

There is communication between you and the computer in *interactive* programs. Describe what you do, and then what the computer does in response, in a program you use. (Example: You enter an answer, and the computer interacts with you by telling you whether your answer is right or wrong.)

What is a blood drive? (an effort to get volunteers to donate blood for transfusions)

Do you know anyone who has volunteered to give blood for *transfusions*? (Ask students who answer "yes" to tell what they know.)

Maybe you are familiar with the word *interference* meaning "the annoying static that comes *between* you and the music you enjoy on the car radio." Why is there often static during a lightning storm? (If lightning strikes close to a radio station, it can *interfere* with reception and contribute to static.)

ASSIGN WRITTEN EXERCISES

Exercise A: Synonyms (page 11)

1. A   2. C   3. D   4. C   5. A

Exercise B: Meaning in Context (page 12)

1. interactive   2. transmit   3. interval   4. intermittent

Exercise C: Extend Your Vocabulary (page 12)

1. C   2. A   3. B   4. Answers will vary.

Reproducible Worksheet: Lesson 3 (page 65 in this book)

LESSON 4: REVIEWING LESSONS 1–3 (PAGES 13–17)

Before your students do the written review exercises in the book, conduct an oral review of the meanings of the featured roots and prefixes, the word parts from the Exercise Cs, and the key vocabulary from Lessons 1, 2, and 3.

DISCUSS

Use these kinds of questions to challenge students.

What is the connection in meaning between the words *equidistant* and *equilateral*? (They both have the *equ* root, which can mean "equal;" *equidistant* means "equal distances from," and *equilateral* means "equal sides on.") Lesson 2

Even though a *circuit* is not round like a circle, how is it related to the root *circ*? (A circuit is a pathway on which electricity can go *around* in an unbroken route, like the unbroken line *around* a circle.) Lesson 1

How do the meanings "between" and "across" overlap in the word *transfer*? (You have to go *across* from one place to another to transfer things *between* two places.) Lesson 3

Think of a three-syllable word that means "to move around." (*circulate*) What part of that word gives you the "around" clue? (the root *circ*) Lesson 1

REINFORCE

What prefixes do you associate with the numbers 1, 2, 3, 4? (*uni-, bi-, tri-, quadr-*) Lessons 1, 2

The word *united* starts with *uni-*. Use *united* in a sentence that shows the "one" connection. (Example: The first thirteen states banded together to become *one* nation, the *United* States of America.) Lesson 1

The word *bilingual* starts with *bi-*. Use *bilingual* in a sentence that shows the "two" connection. (Example: The teacher of the *bilingual* class can speak *two* languages, English and Spanish.) Lesson 1

The word *triceratops* starts with *tri-*. Use *triceratops* in a sentence that shows the "three" connection. (Example: Drawings of the dinosaur *triceratops* show the creature with *three* horns.) Lesson 1

The word *quadruped* starts with *quadr-*. Use *quadruped* in a sentence that shows the "four" connection. (Example: Animals that walk on *four* feet are called *quadruped*s.) Lesson 2

Hand a student a balled-up piece of paper. Tell the student to demonstrate a *lateral* pass.

Ask: Why did you throw to the side? (because *lateral* means "side") Lesson 2

Hold up a pair of scissors. Snip them noisily in the air. Ask: What root comes to mind when I bring the blades of these scissors together? (the root *sect* because it means "cut") Lesson 3

EXPLORE

When students would benefit from a more in-depth exploration of a particular word, the additional word-learning strategies at the beginning of this book (pages vi–viii) can be helpful.

GUIDE ORAL PRACTICE

Activity 1: Definition Challenge

Give each student a card (3" by 5" or 5" by 7"). Assign each student one of the twenty-five words from the box at the top of page 14 in the student book. Have the student copy the complete definition of that word on the card. Line up the class in two teams, facing each other.

The first student on Team A reads a definition. The first student on Team B can earn two points by coming up with the word that fits the definition. If the answer is incorrect, Team B may still earn one point if another member can come up with the word.

The teams take turns until all the definitions have been read. The team with the most points wins.

Activity 2: Charades (sorting by parts of speech)

Hand each student another blank card (3" by 5" or 5" by 7"). Again assign to each student one of the twenty-five words, but make sure it is a different one from the word the student had for Activity 1. The student will copy the new word and its full definition from the book.

Write these categories on the board: nouns, verbs, adjectives, noun and verb. Tell students to sort themselves into these four groups, according to the part of speech of their assigned words. Their groupings should look like this:

Nouns	Verbs	Adjectives	Noun and Verb
circuit	circulate	circular	transfer
cycle	equate	dependent	
cyclone	interfere	equidistant	
equality	intersect	equilateral	
equator	recycle	interactive	
interval	transact	intermittent	
pendulum	transmit	pending	
semicircle			
transfusion			
unicycle			

Let the student holding the word *transfer* move to either the group with nouns or the group with verbs. Tell each group to select two of their words to act out, as in charades. Allow a little time for each group to plan what they will do. All of the group's words should stay on display while the acting is taking place. The other students have to guess which word is being portrayed.

Activity 3: Charades (sorting by syllables)

Have each student give his or her word card from the previous activity to another student. Tell students to sort themselves into new groups, according to the number of syllables in their word. Then, have each group line up in alphabetical order, while holding up their cards. Their groupings should look like this:

Two	Three	Four	Five
circuit	circular	equality	equilateral
cycle	circulate	equidistant	
cyclone	dependent	interactive	
equate	equator	intermittent	
pending	interfere	semicircle	
transact	intersect	unicycle	
transfer	interval		
transmit	pendulum		
	recycle		
	transfusion		

Let the student with the five-syllable word join the four-syllable word group. Proceed as above, with each group planning charades for two words.

ASSIGN WRITTEN EXERCISES
Exercise A: Matching (page 13)

1. D   2. E   3. F   4. C   5. A   6. B

7. J   8. I   9. K   10. H   11. G

12.–14. Sentences will vary.

Exercise B: Sorting (pages 14–15)

1. CIRC	2. CYCL	3. EQU	4. PEND	5. TRANS-	6. INTER-
circuit	unicycle	equidistant	pending	transact	intermittent
circular	cyclone	equality	pendulum	transmit	interfere
semicircle	cycle	equate	dependent	transfusion	interval
circulate	recycle	equator		transfer	interactive
		equilateral			intersect

Answers will vary regarding the words that students add to the lists.

A. 1 and 2   B. 5 and 6   C. "one" and "revolving"   D. "between" and "cut"

Exercise C: Vocabulary from Your Textbooks (page 15)

1. circulate   2. intersect, equilateral   3. circuit   4. interactive

Exercise D: Rhyming Riddles (page 16)

1. C   2. D   3. *A*   4. B

Exercise E: Writing and Discussion Activities (pages 16–17)

Answers will vary.

LESSON 5: LOOKING AT OUR PLANET (PAGES 18–21)

Key Words

aquaculture	aquatic	subterranean	terrain
aquamarine	Mediterranean	terrace	territory

INTRODUCE LESSON 5

(page 18) Introduce Lesson 5 orally by having students read the title "Looking at Our Planet" and the two featured roots *aqua*, meaning "water," and *terr*, meaning "land."

Ask students to name some bodies of water and large areas of land on our planet. (Examples: various continents, seas, and oceans)

What do we call the places where the land and water meet? (the shore, the beach, the coast)

PREVIEW FAMILIAR WORDS

(pages 18, 19) *aquarium, Aquarius, extraterrestrial, terrarium*

Activity 1: *aqua*

Display the familiar words *aquarium* and *Aquarius*. Read them orally and then chorally with the class. Underline the root *aqua* in each one.

Ask students the following questions:

What creatures live in an aquarium? (fish) Can they live on land? (No, fish can live only in *water*.)

People of ancient times thought they saw pictures in the arrangements of some of the stars and gave them names. What is the term for these groupings of stars? (constellation)

The constellation Aquarius, or *water* bearer, got its name because it looked like a person carrying water. The stargazers of long ago divided the year into twelve equal parts and named each part after a different constellation. The names of these constellations became the names for the signs of the zodiac. Does anyone have a birthday between January 21 and February 18? What part of the zodiac is associated with this part of the year? (Aquarius, the *water* bearer)

Ask: What is the shared meaning for the root *aqua* in the words *aquarium* and *Aquarius*? (water)

Activity 2: *terr*

Display the familiar words *extraterrestrial* and *terrarium*. Read them orally and then chorally with the class. Underline the root *terr* in each one.

Ask students the following questions:

Some classrooms or labs have both an aquarium and a terrarium as homes for living creatures. What is the difference between the two homes? (An aquarium is for creatures that live in water. A terrarium is for creatures that live on *land*.)

Describe the movie character that comes to your mind when I say the name ET. (ET was a spindly little creature from another planet.)

What familiar word does ET stand for? (extraterrestrial)

What part of the word *extraterrestrial* means "outside of; beyond"? (the prefix *extra-*)

Could ET thrive in our land? (No, he needed to go home to his planet, his *land.*)

Ask: What is the shared meaning for the root *terr* in *extraterrestrial* and *terrarium*? (land)

PRESENT KEY WORDS

Display the key words. Read them orally and then chorally with the class.

Have the students underline the root in each key word in the box on page 18; then have them check to be sure that their words look like this.

<u>aqua</u>culture	<u>aqua</u>tic	sub<u>ter</u>ranean	<u>ter</u>rain
<u>aqua</u>marine	Medi<u>ter</u>ranean	<u>ter</u>race	<u>ter</u>ritory

Ask students the following questions:

Which words begin with a root? (*aquaculture, aquamarine, aquatic, terrace, terrain, territory*)

In which words does the root *not* appear at the beginning? (*Mediterranean* and *subterranean* start with prefixes. The root *terr* is in the middle.)

On a classroom globe, find and describe the location of the Mediterranean Sea. (It is between the southern part of Europe and the northern part of Africa.)

What is the location of Italy and Greece in relation to the Mediterranean Sea? (They border the Mediterranean Sea to the north.) We are studying Greek and Latin roots in this book. People living in Greece spoke Greek. Who spoke Latin? (the Romans and people living in the countries controlled by Rome)

Why do you think there are so many Greek and Latin roots in the English language? (The Roman Empire, which used the Latin language, extended across Europe and as far as England. So the Spanish, French, and English languages sprang from Greek and Latin roots.)

As students complete the "Using Root Clues" section, encourage them to use the meanings of the roots to find the correct answer. Have them check the columns <u>before</u> they study the complete definitions of the words.

Dictate answers so that students can check themselves.

(page 18) 1. B   2. D   3. C   4. A

Present each key word, paying attention to pronunciation, part of speech, definition with context sentence, and other parts of the listing as applicable (additional derivation, related word form, illustration).

In this lesson, have students focus on the section entitled *Nota Bene.* Remind them that these words from Latin mean "Note well."

Have students turn to page 19, read the *Nota Bene,* and look at the definition, context sentence, and map for the listing of the word *Mediterranean.* What extra information does the *Nota Bene* give about *Mediterranean,* beyond what is given in the listing? (It points out that in the days of the Roman Empire when Latin was spoken, the Mediterranean Sea was thought of as the center of civilization. Also, it indicates that *med,* from *medius,* means "middle.")

Turn back to page 1 and reread the *Nota Bene* at the bottom of that page. What extra information does it give about *circuit,* beyond the definition? (It explains the relationship of the word to the root *circ.*)

What is one purpose of a *Nota Bene?* (to give extra information about a word or root)

GUIDE ORAL PRACTICE
Activity 1: Connections and Examples

Most of the key words that contain the root *terr* have a strong connection with the land. Let's come up with examples of the kinds of land these words refer to.

What are some examples of *subterranean* places? (an underground cave, a mine shaft sunk deep into the ground, miners' tunnels)

What are some examples of *territories?* (the Louisiana Territory, the Northwest Territory)

Both *territory* and *terrain* mean "land" and yet their meanings are slightly different. What is the difference in meaning between these two words? Write the following two sentences on the board, and have students read them.

The explorers made their way across unknown territory.

As we hiked farther up the mountain, the terrain became rockier.

What does land mean when we use the word *territory* and what does land mean when we use the word *terrain?* (*Territory* emphasizes land as a measured area; *terrain* emphasizes the surface details, such as rough, smooth.)

What are some advantages of using terraces to farm a hillside? (They allow people to use land that otherwise could not be cultivated. They help prevent erosion.)

What might be some disadvantages? (It could be difficult to get to, to bring water to, to farm with machines.) How could you create flat areas for planting crops on a hillside?

(You could make steps.) Those steps are called *terraces*. Where else do you see terraces? (in sloping yards where landscapers have put in landings)

One meaning of *terrace* is "a patio." Do you have a terrace with your house? Describe it or some other terraces you have seen.

Activity 2: Draw, Display, Discuss

Find pictures in magazines and books that show the color aquamarine, and display them in the classroom. Ask: What things in the pictures are aquamarine? Do all of the pictures show exactly the same color? (probably not) How would you describe the color of aquamarine? (a mixture of green and blue) There are two meaningful parts in the word *aquamarine: aqua*, meaning "water," and *marine*, meaning "sea." What is the connection between these parts and the color definition? (In some places, seawater is greenish-blue; in others, bluish-green.)

Draw an underwater scene showing a variety of *aquatic* creatures and plants. (Examples: a scuba diver looking at coral, seaweed, anemones, starfish; a goldfish in a bowl with grasses; a bathysphere surrounded by algae and sharks)

What are some products raised by means of aquaculture, which you might see in a supermarket? (various seaweeds, various seafoods like salmon, trout) Why do you think people are using aquaculture? (shortage of fish from overfishing and pollution; easier to control supply)

ASSIGN WRITTEN EXERCISES
Exercise A: Synonyms (page 20)

   1. c   2. d   3. b   4. c   5. a

Exercise B: Meaning in Context (pages 20–21)

   1. Mediterranean   2. terrain   3. aquamarine   4. aquatic

Exercise C: Extend Your Vocabulary (page 21)

   1. D   2. C   3. A   4. B   5. Answers will vary.

Reproducible Worksheet: Lesson 5 (page 66 in this book)

LESSON 6: EXPLORING DISTANT PLACES (PAGES 22–25)

Key Words

astronaut	astronomy	teleconference	telemarketing
astronomical	telecast	telegraph	telescope

INTRODUCE LESSON 6

(page 22) Introduce Lesson 6 orally by having students read the title "Exploring Distant Places" and the two featured roots *tele*, meaning "far away," and *astr*, meaning "star; outer space."

Both *astr* and *tele* carry meanings related to distance. After reading the list of key words, which root do you associate with greater distances? Why? (*astr* because it is connected with outer space and words like astronaut; *tele* is connected with words that express distances mainly on our planet.)

PREVIEW FAMILIAR WORDS

(pages 22, 23) *telephone, television, astronomer, disaster*

Activity 1: *tele*

Display the familiar words *telephone* and *television*. Read them orally and then chorally with the class. Underline the root *tele* in each one.

Ask students the following questions:

Do you know who invented the telephone? (Alexander Graham Bell) Do we still see his name connected to the telephone business? (Yes, there are still phone companies that use the name Bell.)

If I tell you that *phon* means "sound, voice, speech," can you tell me what the parts of the familiar word *telephone* mean exactly or literally? ("*far* away *voice*" from *tele* and *phon*)

Name some of the types of telephones people have used over the years. (dial telephones, party lines, cordless telephones, cell phones, the latest phones equipped with cameras, music, and e-mail)

Do the programs you see on television come from within your home or from some *distant* place? (some *distant* place)

Ask: What are the shared meanings for the root *tele* in the words *telephone* and *television*? (far, distant)

Activity 2: *astr*

Display the familiar words *astronomer* and *disaster*. Read them orally and then chorally with the class. Underline *astr* (or *aster*) in each one. Explain that the Greek root is spelled *aster* and the Latin root is spelled *astr*.

Ask students the following questions:

What is a star? (an object in outer space that gives off light)

What star is closest to our planet Earth? (the sun, which is the *star* of our solar system)

What does it mean to "wish upon a star"? (It means to make a wish, hoping that the *star* has some magical power to make the wish come true.)

What is a disaster? (a terrible event)

Long ago, people believed stars and their positions in the sky could influence people's lives in good ways. Let's look at the parts of the word *disaster*. *Dis-* means "apart from"; *aster* means "star." Why would being "apart from the stars" be a bad thing? (A person is separated from the good influence of the stars.)

What do astronomers study? (planets and *stars*)

Ask: What is the shared meaning for the root *astr* in *astronomer* and *disaster*? (star)

PRESENT KEY WORDS

Display the key words. Read them orally and then chorally with the class.

Have students underline the root in each key word in the box on page 22; then have them check to be sure that their words look like this.

<u>astr</u>onaut	<u>astr</u>onomy	<u>tele</u>conference	<u>tele</u>marketing
<u>astr</u>onomical	<u>tele</u>cast	<u>tele</u>graph	<u>tele</u>scope

How many key words begin with a root? (All eight of them begin with *astr* or *tele*.)

Look at the five words that start with *tele*. In each word, cover *tele*. What words do you have left? (*cast, conference, graph, marketing, scope*)

These base words and/or roots account for part of the meaning of each word. Put together the clues from the root *tele* and the rest of the word to answer these questions:

Which instrument was invented to send messages long distances? (*telegraph*)

Which is a television program? (*telecast*)

As students complete the "Using Root Clues" section, encourage them to use the meanings of the roots to find the correct answer. Have them match the columns <u>before</u> they study the complete definitions of the words.

Dictate answers so that students can check themselves.

(page 22) 1. D   2. C   3. A   4. B

Present each key word, paying attention to pronunciation, part of speech, definition with context sentence, and other parts of the listing as applicable (additional derivation, related word form, illustration).

In this lesson, only one of the words on pages 22–24 is listed with more than one meaning. Which one? (*astronomical*) Which meaning of *astronomical* is synonymous with *tremendous*? (the first meaning, "extremely large, huge.") How do you know? (That synonym can take the place of *astronomical* in the context sentence for the first definition, but not for the second.)

What part of speech are both meanings of *astronomical*? (adjectives)

GUIDE ORAL PRACTICE

Activity 1: Connections and Examples

Look at the word *teleconference.*

What word that means "to talk" do you see in the middle of *teleconference*? (*confer*)

What longer word do you see in *teleconference* that means "a meeting where people talk"? (*conference*)

Suppose the people who want to *confer* at a *conference* are in different cities. How can they arrange to talk? (They can get on phones in their different cities and get connected for a teleconference.)

Look at the key words that start with *astr.*

Which word is a person who travels away from our planet? (*astronaut*)

Which is a branch of science? (*astronomy*)

How big is "astronomical"? Ask students to give you other words that mean very large; write these and *astronomical* on the board. (Examples: *huge, massive, tremendous, gigantic, colossal, immense, enormous, vast, astronomical*) After you have from eight to ten words, ask students to make a "word line," arranging the words in a gradation from the "smallest" big to the "largest" big. Then compare their results. Do not expect consensus. The discussion may lead to connecting *vast* with space, *massive* with weight, density, or heaviness, and *colossal* with abstract concepts such as *blunder.*

Activity 2: Draw, Display, Discuss

Discuss current news articles about and pictures of astronauts. Display some of them in the classroom.

Discuss experiences with telemarketing (phone calls at dinner time, the do-not-call list), telescopes (in backyard, at planetariums), and teleconferencing (what do students know?).

From previous class work in astronomy (if applicable), draw the solar system.

ASSIGN WRITTEN EXERCISES

Exercise A: Synonyms (page 24)

1. b   2. a   3. d   4. c   5. d

Exercise B: Meaning in Context (page 25)

1. telecast   2. astronaut   3. telescope   4. teleconference   5. astronomy

Exercise C: Extend Your Vocabulary (page 25)

1. B   2. D   3. A   4. C

Below the illustrations, students should write:

5. periscope   6. microscope   7. ophthalmoscope   8. kaleidoscope

Reproducible Worksheet: Lesson 6 (page 67 in this book)

LESSON 7: CHANGING MEANING WITH PREFIXES (PAGES 26–31)

Key Words

inactive	insomnia	semiconscious
informal	semiannual	semiformal
insignificant	semicolon	semiprecious

INTRODUCE LESSON 7

(page 26) Introduce Lesson 7 orally by having students read the title "Changing Meaning with Prefixes" and the two featured prefixes *semi-*, meaning "half" or "partly," and *in-*, meaning "not."

Remind students that in Lesson 1, they met the word *semicircle*. What does it mean? (half circle). In Lesson 2, they met the word *dependent*, which means "needing help." What word could be used to describe someone who does *not* need help? (*independent*)

PREVIEW FAMILIAR WORDS

(pages 27, 28) *incomplete, inconvenient, incorrect, infrequent, semifinal semiprivate, semisweet*

Activity 1: *in-*

Display the familiar words *incomplete, inconvenient, incorrect, infrequent.* Read them orally and then chorally with the class. Underline the prefix *in-* on each one.

Ask students these questions:

When I cover the prefix *in-* on each familiar word, what is left? (four words: *complete, convenient, correct,* and *frequent*)

To change the meaning of "complete" to "not complete," what do I do? (Add the prefix *in-* to form the word *incomplete,* which means "not complete.")

Does the prefix *in-* have the same effect on the words *convenient, correct,* and *frequent?* (Yes, it changes them to *inconvenient* meaning "not convenient," *incorrect* meaning "not correct," and *infrequent* meaning "not frequent.")

Ask: What is the shared meaning for the prefix *in-* on *incomplete, inconvenient, incorrect,* and *infrequent?* (not)

Activity 2: *semi-*

Display the familiar words *semifinal, semiprivate,* and *semisweet.*

Read them orally and then chorally with the class. Underline the prefix *semi-* in each one.

Ask students the following questions:

In a tournament, how many teams compete in the final game? (two)

Before the field is narrowed down to just two teams, there are four teams that have made it a good *part* of the way to the finals. What familiar word would you call the games between the four teams? (*semifinal*)

If you visit a friend in a private room at the hospital, how many patients would be in the room? (one)

Which familiar word would you use for the room if two patients were in it, each occupying *half* of the room? (*semiprivate*)

Chocolate can range from very sweet to very bitter. Which familiar word describes chocolate that has been mixed with some, but not a lot of, sugar? (*semisweet*) Yes, chocolate can be *partly* sweetened.

Ask: What is the shared meaning for the prefix *semi-* in the words *semifinal, semiprivate,* and *semisweet?* (partly or half)

PRESENT KEY WORDS.

Display the key words. Read them orally and then chorally with the class.

Have students underline the prefix in each key word in the box on page 26; then have them check to be sure that the words look like this.

<u>in</u>active	<u>in</u>significant	<u>semi</u>annual	<u>semi</u>conscious	<u>semi</u>precious
<u>in</u>formal	<u>in</u>somnia	<u>semi</u>colon	<u>semi</u>formal	

There are nine key words in Lesson 7. How many begin with a prefix? (all nine)

Maybe you know the meanings of some of the base words and/or roots to which the prefixes are added. Look at the first three: *inactive, informal, insignificant.* What base words do you have when you cover the prefix *in-?* (*active, formal, significant*)

What does each base word mean? (Note students' definitions on the board and refine, if necessary.)

How does the prefix *in-* change the meaning of each of these words? (As with the familiar words, *in-* adds the meaning "not," so the meanings of the words become "not active," "not formal," "not significant.")

One of the key words means "not sleeping." The condition of being unable to sleep is called *insomnia.* Which part of the word means "not"? (the prefix *in-*)

As students complete the "Using Prefix Clues" section, encourage them to use the meanings of the prefixes to find the correct answer. Have them match the columns <u>before</u> they study the complete definitions of the words.

Dictate answers so that students can check themselves.

(page 26) 1. D   2. A   3. C   4. B

Present each key word, paying attention to pronunciation, part of speech, definition with context sentence, and other parts of the listing as applicable (additional derivation, related word form, illustration).

Use the *Nota Bene* about *in*, at the bottom of page 27, to make the important point that a prefix can have more than one meaning. It may also be a word in itself or it may have no significance on its own. What looks like a prefix may just be the first few letters in a word. Remind students that a prefix changes the meaning of the word to which it is attached.

Ask: In which word is *in* a prefix: *inches* or *incapable*? (*incapable*)

To apply that information to other prefixes, ask:

What does the prefix *un-* usually mean, as in *uncomfortable*? (not) What does *un-* mean in the word *untie*? (reverse the action)

What does the prefix *dis-* usually mean, as in *distrust*? (not) What does *dis-* mean in the word *disappear*? (do the opposite of)

GUIDE ORAL PRACTICE

Activity 1: Connections and Examples

You may discover that you have previous associations with some key words, which help you make connections to their meanings.

Which two words lead you to think of clothes? (*informal* and *semiformal*)

Which word do you associate with gemstones for jewelry? (*semiprecious*)

Which key word do you associate with punctuation? (*semicolon*)

When you are awake, you are conscious. But just before you fall asleep, when you are only *partly* awake, what are you? (*semiconscious*)

Look at the key word *semiannual*. An annual event happens only once a year. What are some annual events? (birthdays, holidays, graduations)

What are some events that happen every six months, every *half* year, *semiannual* events? (Answers will vary. Examples: the spring and fall awards assemblies at school, standardized tests at six-month intervals, dental or health appointments)

Activity 2: Draw, Display, Discuss

Who has a piece of jewelry with a gemstone (perhaps a birthstone) in it? Have students identify the semiprecious birthstones for their birthday months. Make a list of the gemstones and their colors. (January: garnet, deep red; February: amethyst, blue, and so on)

Who has attended a wedding? Who has participated in a wedding? What did you do? What did you wear? Did you wear formal or semiformal clothes?

Display and discuss pictures of formal, semiformal, and informal clothes.

Draw your favorite outfit. Is it formal, semiformal, or informal?

ASSIGN WRITTEN EXERCISES
Exercise A: Synonyms (pages 28–29)

1. b   2. b   3. d   4. b   5. a

Exercise B: Meaning in Context (page 29)

1. insignificant   2. insomnia   3. semiannual   4. inactive

Exercise C: Extend Your Vocabulary (pages 29–31)

IG-	IL-	IM-	IR-
ignoble	illiterate	impatient	irregular
	illogical	immovable	irreplaceable
		immature	irremovable
		imperfect	irresponsible
		impractical	

1. 1   2. 2   3. 5   4. 4

5. not   6. not   7. not   8. not

9. Answers will vary. Examples: unable, dislike, nonparticipant.

10. Sentences will vary.

Reproducible Worksheet: Lesson 7 (page 68 in this book)

LESSON 8: REVIEWING LESSONS 5–7 (PAGES 32–35)

Before your students do the written review exercises in the book, conduct an oral review of the meanings of the featured roots and prefixes, the word parts from the Exercise Cs, and the key vocabulary from Lessons 5, 6, and 7.

DISCUSS

Use these kinds of questions to challenge students.

What is the connection in meaning between the words *territory* and *subterranean*? (They both have the *terr* root, which can mean "land;" *territory* means "a large region of land," and *subterranean* means "beneath the land.") Lesson 5

Since *inactive* means "not active," why doesn't *inland* mean "not land"? (The prefix *in-* has more than one meaning. It frequently means "not," but it can also mean "within," as in *inland*. An inland village is within the land, not on the coast.) Lesson 7

What meaning does *tele* carry? (distant) Which *tele* word do you associate with a greater distance: *telemarketing* or *telescope*? (A telescope enables people to see objects in outer space. Telemarketing is limited to this planet.) Lesson 6

Think of a four-syllable word that means "half awake." (*semiconscious*) What part of that word gives you the "half" clue? (the prefix *semi-*) Lesson 7

REINFORCE

What words in this sentence are derived from the root *marin*: The mariner took his boat out from the marina and collected marine plants. (mariner, marina, marine) Lesson 5

Explain how the meaning of each is connected to the root *marin*, meaning "sea." (A mariner is a sailor who works on the sea. A marina is a place by the sea where boats or ships dock. A marine plant is one that lives in the sea.) Lesson 5

Most words that end in *scope* refer to instruments used for looking. But there is one common scope that your doctor uses for listening. When you have a cold and the doctor listens to your chest, what instrument does he or she use? (stethoscope) Lesson 6

Think of a sentence that shows the "instrument" connection for *microscope*. (Example: I put a hair on a slide and looked at it through the lens of a microscope.) Lesson 6

What materials are needed to build a *periscope*? (mirrors and a tube) Building a periscope is a possible project for students. Lesson 6

What are some of the various spellings for the prefix *in-*? Give a word for each. (Examples: *ir-* as in *irresponsible*, *im-* as in *impossible*, *il-* as in *illegal*, and *ig-* as in *ignoble*) Lesson 7

EXPLORE

When students would benefit from a more in-depth exploration of a particular word, the additional word-learning strategies at the beginning of this book (pages vi–viii) can be helpful.

GUIDE ORAL PRACTICE

Activity 1: Definition Challenge

Give each student a card (3" by 5" or 5" by 7"). Assign each student one of the twenty-five words from the box at the bottom of page 32 in the student book. Have the student copy the complete definition of that word on the card. Line up the class in two teams, facing each other.

The first student on Team A reads a definition. The first student on Team B can earn two points by coming up with the word that fits the definition. If the answer is incorrect, Team B may still earn one point if another member can come up with the word.

The teams take turns until all the definitions have been read. The team with the most points wins.

Activity 2: Charades (sorting by parts of speech)

Hand each student another blank card (3" by 5" or 5" by 7"). Again assign to each student one of the twenty-five words, but make sure it is a different one from the word the student had for Activity 1. The student will copy the new word and its full definition from the book.

Write these two categories on the board: nouns and adjectives. Tell students to sort themselves into these two groups, according to the part of speech of their assigned words. Their groupings should look like this:

Nouns	Adjectives
aquaculture	aquamarine
astronaut	aquatic
astronomy	astronomical
insomnia	inactive
semicolon	informal
telecast	insignificant
teleconference	Mediterranean
telegraph	semiannual
telemarketing	semiconscious
telescope	semiformal
terrace	semiprecious
terrain	subterranean
territory	

Tell each group to select two of their words to act out, as in charades. Allow a little time for each group to plan the charades. All of the group's words should stay on display while the acting is taking place. The other students have to guess which word is being portrayed.

Activity 3: Charades (sorting by syllables)

Have each student give his or her word card from the previous activity to another student. Tell students to sort themselves into new groups, according to the number of syllables in their word. Then, have each group line up in alphabetical order, while holding up their cards. Their groupings should look like this:

Two	Three	Four	Five	Six
terrace	aquatic	aquaculture	astronomical	Mediterranean
terrain	astronaut	aquamarine	insignificant	
	inactive	astronomy	semiannual	
	informal	insomnia	subterranean	
	telecast	semicolon	teleconference	
	telegraph	semiconscious	telemarketing	
	telescope	semiformal		
		semiprecious		
		territory		

Reduce to three groups by having the six-syllable word join the five-syllable word group, and by combining the two-syllable and three-syllable word groups. Proceed as above, with each group planning charades for two words.

ASSIGN WRITTEN EXERCISES
Exercise A: Matching (page 32)

1. F	2. B	3. A	4. E	5. D
6. C	7. I	8. G	9. H	10. G.

Exercise B: Sorting (pages 32–33)

1. AQUA	**2. TERR**	**3. ASTR**
aquaculture	territory	astronaut
aquamarine	Mediterranean	astronomy
aquatic	terrain	astronomical
	subterranean	
	terrace	

4. TELE	**5. IN-**	**6. SEMI-**
telecast	informal	semicolon
telescope	insignificant	semiformal
telegraph	insomnia	semiconscious
teleconference	inactive	semiannual
telemarketing		semiprecious

Answers will vary regarding the words that students add to the lists.

A. 3 and 4

B. 6

C. "distant" and "instrument for seeing"

D. "water" and "of the sea"

Exercise C: Vocabulary from Your Textbooks (page 34)

1. semicolon   2. telescope and astronomical   3. semiprecious   4. telegraph

Exercise D: Rhyming Riddles (page 34)

1. B   2. A   3. C   4. E   5. D

Exercise E: Writing and Discussion Activities (page 35)

Answers will vary.

LESSON 9: CREATING ORDER (PAGES 36–39)

Key Words

civics	civilian	coordinate	ordinarily
civil	civility	extraordinary	uncivilized

INTRODUCE LESSON 9

(page 36) Introduce Lesson 9 orally by having students read the title "Creating Order" and the two featured roots *civi*, meaning "relating to citizens," and *ord*, meaning "regular."

Ask students to name characteristics they associate with civilized societies. (Answers will vary but may include laws, educational systems, organized government, art, people living in orderly, peaceful ways.) Reinforce the ideas that *civi*lization imposes *ord*er and that *citizens* have some *regularity* in their lives.

How does disorder in a country affect the lives of the citizens? (Examples: The orderly delivery of food to markets can be disrupted. Planes, trains, and buses may not run on schedule. Innocent citizens can be injured or even killed in disasters or riots.)

PREVIEW FAMILIAR WORDS

(pages 36, 38) *civilization, civilize, disorder, order, orderly, orderliness, reorder*

Activity 1: *civi*

Display the familiar words *civilization* and *civilize*. Read them orally and then chorally with the class. Underline the root *civi* in each one.

Ask students the following questions:

There are a number of books about children who were raised by animals in a jungle (Tarzan from the series by Edgar Rice Burroughs, Mowgli from the books by Rudyard Kipling). When these children left the jungle to live with human beings were they considered civilized? (usually no) Why not? What are some of the differences between how animals live and how humans live? (As humans began living a settled life and formed cities of which they were *citizens*, they developed laws, language, art, music, and tools that made their lives different from those of animals.)

What evidence can you still see in Italy of the ancient civilization that flourished there when Latin was spoken? (Some frescos, pieces of pottery, paintings, and statues from ancient Rome have been preserved; this evidence shows us that the *citizens* of Rome enjoyed a level of civilization that supported the arts. In the Mediterranean area, people had gradually moved from a wandering nomadic existence into villages, towns, and finally cities. The Romans and the Greeks had achieved a level of civilization where order prevailed, and where art and science could flourish.)

Ask: What is the shared meaning for the root *civi* in the words *civilization* and *civilize*? (citizen, member of a city)

Activity 2: *ord*

Display the familiar words *disorder, order, orderly, orderliness, reorder.* Read them orally and then chorally with the class. Underline the root *ord* in each one.

Ask students the following questions:

What are some examples of disorder? (a messy room, people not following traffic rules, people speaking out of turn at a meeting)

Which of the familiar words is the antonym of *disorder?* (order)

Let's look at another meaning of *order.* How are *order* and *reorder* connected? (Order means to send away for something and reorder means to do it again.)

Compose a sentence in which *order* is a noun. (Example: The judge wanted order in the courtroom.) Compose a sentence in which *order* is a verb. (Example: We ordered sandwiches for lunch.)

Describe a classroom that is orderly, where orderliness prevails. (In the discussion, emphasize *regularity* of schedule, rules, behavior.)

Ask: What is the shared meaning for the root *ord* in *disorder, order, orderly, orderliness, reorder?* (regular)

PRESENT KEY WORDS

Display the key words. Read them orally and then chorally with the class.

Have students underline the root in each key word in the box on page 36; then have them check to be sure that their words look like this.

<u>civ</u>ics	<u>civ</u>ilian	co<u>ord</u>inate	<u>ord</u>inarily
<u>civ</u>il	<u>civ</u>ility	extra<u>ord</u>inary	un<u>civ</u>ilized

Which words begin with a root? (*civics, civil, civilian, civility, ordinarily*)

In which words does the root *not* appear at the beginning? (*coordinate, extraordinary, uncivilized*) What prefixes do you see on these words? (*co-, extra-, un-*)

Which of these prefixes (*co-, extra-, un-*) did you meet in a previous lesson on negative prefixes? (*un-*) What does *un-* mean? (not) So what does *uncivilized* mean? (not civilized)

You have seen the prefix *extra-* before, in the word *extraterrestrial.* What does the prefix *extra-* mean? (beyond or more than) So what does *extraordinary* mean? (beyond or more than ordinary) Describe some sights or events that are extraordinary. (Examples: natural wonders like Old Faithful geyser at Yellowstone National Park;

impressive structures like the Lincoln Memorial; fireworks, parades)

You will study the prefix *co-* as in *coordinate* in a future lesson. It can mean "together or with."

As students complete the "Using Root Clues" section, encourage them to use the meanings of the roots to find the correct answer. Have them match the columns <u>before</u> they study the complete definitions of the words.

Dictate answers so that students can check themselves.

(page 36) 1. B   2. D   3. A   4. C

Present each key word, paying attention to pronunciation, part of speech, definition with context sentence, and other parts of the listing as applicable (additional derivation, related word form, illustration).

On page 37, read the complete listings for the words *civil* (at top) and *uncivilized* (at bottom). What part of speech are both words? (adjectives) How many definitions do you see for each word? (two definitions for each)

Which pair of definitions show more strongly that the words *civil* and *uncivilized* are antonyms? (the second pair, since *civil* is defined as "courteous," and *uncivilized* is defined as "acting without courtesy")

GUIDE ORAL PRACTICE

Activity 1: Connections and Examples

The adjective *civil* and the noun *civility* are related. *Civil* means "fairly polite and courteous." *Civility* is "the act of being fairly polite and courteous." Have a student demonstrate an enthusiastic greeting, and then a civil greeting. (Example: The enthusiastic greeting, with a big smile, might be, "Hi, it's great to see you," while the civil greeting might be a minimal, "Hello.")

Draw a Venn diagram on the board. Label one circle "civilian," the other circle "military," and the overlapping area of the circles "both." Ask: What are the differences in meaning between the two words? What are the similarities? Encourage students to think about who is in the military, where they live, work, and so on.

Courses that teach about *civics* (a citizen's rights and duties) have many names. What are some of these names? (social studies, government, political science, citizenship, history)

What is the name of the course at our school that teaches about the responsibilities of citizens? (Answers will vary.)

Activity 2: Draw, Display, Discuss

Draw an *extraordinary* creature or vehicle. Explain why it is extraordinary.

What do you do *ordinarily* on Saturdays? (Answers should include some regularly scheduled activities.) Have you ever had an extraordinary Saturday when what you did was completely different? Describe that Saturday.

Compare and contrast the extended meanings of *civil* as in Civil War and civil rights.

ASSIGN WRITTEN EXERCISES

Exercise A: Antonyms (page 38)

1. b   2. c   3. d   4. a   5. c

Exercise B: Meaning in Context (page 39)

1. civics   2. coordinated   3. civil   4. extraordinary

Exercise C: Extend Your Vocabulary (page 39)

1. active   2. possible   3. vital   4. original   5. creative   6. Sentences will vary.

Reproducible Worksheet: Lesson 9 (page 69 in this book)

LESSON 10: MEASURING IN MATH AND SCIENCE (PAGES 40–43)

> ## Key Words
>
> diameter   metronome   symmetrical   thermometer
>
> geometry   perimeter   thermal   thermostat

INTRODUCE LESSON 10

(page 40) Introduce Lesson 10 orally by having students read the title "Measuring in Math and Science" and the two featured roots *metr/meter,* meaning "measurement," and *therm,* meaning "heat."

These two roots form the name of an instrument that *measures heat.* What is it? (the thermometer)

Fahrenheit and Celsius are two scales for measuring temperature. Most countries use the Celsius scale. Which scale is used in the United States? (the Fahrenheit). What do you know about these two scales? (As students generate information about the two scales write it on the board. You can provide information that they do not. The Celsius scale is metric in that it is divided into 100 units, 0 degrees being the freezing point of water and 100 degrees being the boiling point of water. With the Fahrenheit scale, water boils at 212 degrees and freezes at 32 degrees.)

Which measurement scale appears on our classroom thermometer or the thermometer on the playground? (probably Fahrenheit)

PREVIEW FAMILIAR WORDS

(pages 40, 41) *meter, metric, thermos*

Activity 1: *metr/meter*

Display the familiar words *meter* and *metric.* Read them orally and then chorally with the class. Underline the root *meter/metr* in each one.

Ask students the following questions:

In what subject do you study the metric system? (math)

What are some examples of metric measurement? (centimeter, kilometer, and so on)

What is the unit for *measurement* of length in the metric system? (the meter)

How long is a meter? (39.37 inches)

What measurement is closest to this in the nonmetric system? (a yard, which is 36 inches)

What are some other kinds of meters? (gas, electric, parking)

What do they measure? (the quantity of gas or electricity used; the length of time one uses the space)

Ask: What are the shared meanings for the root *meter/metr* in the words *meter* and *metric?* (measurement)

Activity 2: *therm*

Display the familiar word *thermos*. Read it orally and then chorally with the class. Underline *therm* in thermos.

Ask: What does a thermos do? (It retains *heat* (or cold). It keeps a liquid at the temperature it was when put in the container.)

Ask: What is the meaning for the root *therm* in *thermos?* (heat)

PRESENT KEY WORDS

Display the key words. Read them orally and then chorally with the class.

Have students underline the root in each key word in the box on page 40; then have them check to be sure that their words look like this.

| diameter | metronome | symmetrical | thermometer |
| geometry | perimeter | thermal | thermostat |

Which key words contain the root *therm?* (*thermal, thermometer, thermostat*)

On each of these words, where does the root appear? (at the beginning of the word)

Only one of the key words with the *meter/metr* root has that root in the initial position. Which one? (*metronome*)

As students complete the "Using Root Clues" section, encourage them to use the meanings of the roots to find the correct answer. Have them match the columns before they study the complete definitions of the words.

Dictate answers so that students can check themselves.

(page 40) 1. B   2. A   3. D   4. C

Present each key word, paying attention to pronunciation, part of speech, definition with context sentence, and other parts of the listing as applicable (additional derivation, related word form, illustration).

On pages 40–41, which words have additional meaningful parts that are derived from Greek? (*diameter, geometry, perimeter, symmetrical*)

In *geometry*, what is the Greek root and its meaning? (*ge*, meaning "earth") What other words can you think of that start with *ge* or *geo* and have "earth" connections? (Examples: *geography* which is the study of places on the surface of the earth, and *geology* which is the study of physical features of the earth's crust and interior)

GUIDE ORAL PRACTICE
Activity 1: Connections and Examples

Which three words are names for instruments of measurement? (*thermometer, thermostat,* and *metronome*)

What is the difference between a thermometer and a thermostat? (one tells you what the temperature is and the other regulates the temperature)

What does a metronome measure? (It provides a regulated beat.)

Geometry is not an instrument; it is a subject you study in school. Which key words are connected with geometry? (*diameter, perimeter, symmetrical*)

Activity 2: Draw, Display, Discuss

Display a variety of thermometers to the class. Ask: What is the purpose of each thermometer? (An oral or ear thermometer can be used to take a person's temperature and see if the person has fever. An outdoor thermometer is used to determine the temperature of the air. An oven thermometer helps the cook determine when a turkey or a roast is done.)

Have a student draw a circle on the board. Then say: Draw the diameter of the circle. Assuming it is done correctly, ask: What do you call the two half circles you have made? (semicircles)

Have a student walk around the four sides of the classroom. Ask: Which key word did the walk demonstrate? (*perimeter*)

Ask students to cut out a design from a paper they have folded in half. Display these in the front of the room. Discuss how they are alike and different. (Paper color and texture may be the same, each will be symmetrical within itself, and each design will be different from the others.)

ASSIGN WRITTEN EXERCISES
Exercise A: Synonyms (page 42)

1. c   2. b   3. c   4. d   5. a

Exercise B: Meaning in Context (pages 42–43)

1. thermal   2. thermometer   3. geometry   4. perimeter

Exercise C: Extend Your Vocabulary (page 43)

1. heavier   2. lighter   3. less   4. more

5. D   6. A   7. B   8. C

Reproducible Worksheet: Lesson 10 (page 70 in this book)

LESSON 11: PULLING TOGETHER (PAGES 44–48)

Key Words

construction	extract	retract
contraction	protractor	structure
destructive	reconstruct	traction

INTRODUCE LESSON 11

(page 44) Introduce Lesson 11 orally by having students read the title "Pulling Together" and the two featured roots *struct*, meaning "build," and *tract*, meaning "pull, drag." These roots are found in many words related to doing heavy work and building. They are also used in words connected with thinking and feeling such as *instruction*, *constructive*, *destructive*, *attraction*.

PREVIEW FAMILIAR WORDS

(pages 44, 45) *construct, instruct, instructions, attract, subtract, subtraction, tractor*

Activity 1: *struct*

Display the familiar words *construct, instruct, instructions*. Read them orally and then chorally with the class. Underline the root *struct* in each one.

Ask students these questions:

Which familiar word has exactly the same meaning as the root? (*construct*, which means "build")

What is being built when we use the words *instruct* and *instructions*? (These words are connected with *building* knowledge.)

Ask: What is the shared meaning for the root *struct* in *construct*, *instruct*, and *instructions*? (build)

Activity 2: *tract*

Display the familiar words *attract, subtract, subtraction, tractor.*

Read them orally and then chorally with the class. Underline the root *tract* in each one.

Ask students the following questions:

What is happening in subtraction that is related to the idea of pulling or dragging? (We are pulling away some part of a whole when we subtract something.)

When you put a magnet near paper clips, what happens? (The magnet *attracts* the paper clips; they are *pulled* toward the magnet.)

Name some things that are *pulled* by a tractor. (plows, combines, and other kinds of farm machinery, wagons, trailers, and so on)

Ask: What is the shared meaning for the root *tract* in the words *attract*, *subtract*, *subtraction*, *tractor*? (pull)

PRESENT KEY WORDS

Display the key words. Read them orally and then chorally with the class.

Have students underline the root in each key word in the box on page 44; then have them check to be sure that the words look like this.

con<u>struct</u>ion   de<u>struct</u>ive   pro<u>tract</u>or   re<u>tract</u>   <u>tract</u>ion

con<u>tract</u>ion   ex<u>tract</u>   recon<u>struct</u>   <u>struct</u>ure

Ask students the following questions:

Of the nine key words in Lesson 11, how many begin with a root? (only two: *structure* and *traction*)

What prefixes do you see on the other key words? (*con-* on *construction* and *contraction*, *de-* on *destructive*, *ex-* on *extract*, *pro-* on *protractor*, and *re-* on *reconstruct* and *retract*)

You will meet the prefix *ex-* in Exercise C of this lesson. Try to predict the meaning of *ex-* as in *export*. (out)

You will meet the prefix *re-* in a future lesson. It can mean "again" or "back."

Which meaning does it have in the word *rebuild*? (again)

Which meaning does it have in *return*? (back)

As students complete the "Using Root Clues" section, encourage them to use the meanings of the roots to find the correct answer. Have them match the columns <u>before</u> they study the complete definitions of the words.

Dictate answers so that students can check themselves

(page 44) 1. C   2. A   3. D   4. B

Present each key word, paying attention to pronunciation, part of speech, definition with context sentence, and other parts of the listing as applicable (additional derivation, related word form, illustration).

On page 45, read the complete listing of *extract*. How many definitions? (three: two verb definitions and one noun definition) Inside the parentheses you see the verb pronunciation and the noun pronunciation. How are they different? (When *extract* is used as a verb, the accent is on the second syllable. When *extract* is used as a noun, the accent is on the first syllable.) For further pronunciation practice, have students compose and recite orally sentences in which *extract* is used as both a noun and a verb.

GUIDE ORAL PRACTICE
Activity 1: Connections and Examples

You may notice that you already have associations with some of the key words.

Which word do you associate with building things? (*construction*)

Which word could describe a cyclone that destroys homes? (*destructive*)

Which word do you associate with an apostrophe? (*contraction*) Give examples of contractions. (isn't, wasn't, doesn't, don't, won't, I'll, she's, shouldn't, and others)

Why has reconstruction been very important in the sections of cities that have many old buildings? (In those sections, you can see buildings that may have been constructed one hundred years ago. Without reconstruction, they would not be habitable today.)

Who can describe a time they experienced a loss of *traction*? (Let several students describe their experiences.)

How do doctors use traction? (Ask students to describe medical traction that they have seen or experienced.)

Activity 2: Draw, Display, Discuss

Display, or have a student display, a protractor. Show how this plastic tool is used to draw and measure angles in math. What word describes the shape of a protractor? (*semicircular*)

Display a bottle of extract (vanilla, almond, lemon). Tell what is in the bottle. (liquid flavoring) How much do you use? (a small amount) Why? (The liquid is very concentrated.)

On plain pieces of paper, ask students to draw an illustration of a structure. When they finish, display the drawings and talk about what they show. Most students will probably draw some kind of building. Talk about structures that we can touch. If no one represents abstract structures (as in the structure of sentences, of musical compositions, of ideas), ask students about these. In what way are abstract structures different from concrete structures? Ask them to describe a structure that cannot be touched.

On an airplane flight, not long after takeoff, when the pilot retracts the airplane wheels, what is happening with the wheels? (A mechanism pulls them back inside the body of the plane.)

ASSIGN WRITTEN EXERCISES
Exercise A: Antonyms (page 46)

1. d   2. b   3. c   4. b   5. a

Exercise B: Meaning in Context (page 47)

1. destructive

2. reconstruct

3. structure

4. protractor

5. traction

Exercise C: Extend Your Vocabulary (pages 47–48)

1. B	2. D	3. A	4. C	5. Sentences will vary.
6. D	7. C	8. B	9. A	10. Sentences will vary.

Reproducible Worksheet: Lesson 11 (page 71 in this book)

LESSON 12: REVIEWING LESSONS 9–11 (PAGES 49–53)

Before your students do the written review exercises in the book, conduct an oral review of the meanings of the featured roots and prefixes, the word parts from the Exercise Cs, and the key vocabulary from Lessons 9, 10, and 11.

DISCUSS

Use these kinds of questions to challenge students.

What is the connection in meaning between the words *ordinarily* and *extraordinary?* (They both have the *ord* root, which can mean "regular;" *ordinarily* means "in a regular manner," and *extraordinary* means "beyond the regular.") Lesson 9

How do the prefixes *con-* and *de-* affect the meaning of the words *construction* and *destruction?* (They make the words opposite in meaning. Construction is building up; destruction is tearing down.) Lesson 11

What meaning does the root *meter* have? (measurement) Explain how measurement is involved with each of these words: *diameter, perimeter,* and *thermometer.* (A diameter is the measurement across a circle through its center. A perimeter is the measurement around the outside boundary of an area. A thermometer is an instrument that measures the temperature of a person or a thing.) Lesson 10

Meter, in addition to being a root, is also a word in itself. It is the name for the basic unit of measurement in the metric system. Is a meter shorter or longer than a yard? (a little longer, 39.37 inches; a yard is 36 inches) Lesson 10

Remember that the adjective *civil* means reasonably polite. What suffix do you use to form the noun? (The noun suffix *-ity* makes the noun *civility.*) Lesson 9

REINFORCE

Name measurements in the metric system that use the prefixes *kilo-* and *milli-.* (kilometer, millimeter, kilogram, milligram, kiloliter, milliliter) Both *kilo-* and *milli-* are connected with "thousand." What is the difference? (A kilogram is one thousand grams; a milligram is one-thousandth of a gram.) Lesson 10

What is the adjective form for the noun *possibility?* (*possible*) How about the noun *reality?* (*real*; point out the change in the pronunciation from the noun form with four syllables to the adjective form with one syllable) Lesson 9

Ask students to demonstrate *exhaling, exiting,* and *erasing.* Show the "out" connection of each word. (When exhaling, a person breathes air out. When exiting a room, a person walks out. When erasing a chalkboard, a person rubs out what is written on it.) Lesson 11

EXPLORE

When students would benefit from a more in-depth exploration of a particular word, the additional word-learning strategies at the beginning of this book (pages vi–viii) can be helpful.

GUIDE ORAL PRACTICE
Activity 1: Definition Challenge

Give each student a card (3" by 5" or 5" by 7"). Assign each student one of the twenty-five words from the box at the top of page 50 in the student book. Have the student copy the complete definition of that word on the card. Line up the class in two teams, facing each other.

The first student on Team A reads a definition. The first student on Team B can earn two points by coming up with the word that fits the definition. If the answer is incorrect, Team B may still earn one point if another member can come up with the word.

The teams take turns until all the definitions have been read. The team with the most points wins.

Activity 2: Charades (sorting by parts of speech)

Hand each student another blank card (3" by 5" or 5" by 7"). Again assign to each student one of the twenty-five words, but make sure it is a different one from the word the student had for Activity 1. The student will copy the new word and its full definition from the book.

Write these categories on the board: nouns, verbs, adjectives, adverb, noun and verb. Tell students to sort themselves into these five groups, according to the part of speech of their assigned words. Their groupings should look like this:

Nouns	Verbs	Adjectives	Adverb	Noun and Verb
civics	coordinate	civil	ordinarily	extract
civilian	reconstruct	destructive		
civility	retract	extraordinary		
construction		symmetrical		
contraction		thermal		
diameter		uncivilized		
geometry				
metronome				
perimeter				
protractor				
structure				
thermometer				
thermostat				
traction				

Have the three smallest groups (verbs, adverb, noun and verb) combine, and split the noun group in half. Then tell each of the four groups to select two of their words to act out, as in charades. Allow a little time for each group to plan the charades. All of the group's words should stay on display while the acting is taking place. The other students have to guess which word is being portrayed.

Activity 3: Charades (sorting by syllables)

Have each student give his or her word card from the previous activity to another student. Tell students to sort themselves into new groups, according to the number of syllables in their word. Then, have each group line up in alphabetical order, while holding up their cards. Their groupings should look like this:

Two	**Three**	**Four**	**Five**
civics	civilian	civility	extraordinary
civil	construction	coordinate	ordinarily
extract	contraction	diameter	
retract	destructive	geometry	
structure	metronome	perimeter	
thermal	protractor	symmetrical	
traction	reconstruct	thermometer	
	thermostat	uncivilized	

Reduce to three groups by having the five-syllable and two-syllable word groups combine. Proceed as above, with each group planning charades for two words.

ASSIGN WRITTEN EXERCISES
Exercise A: Matching (page 49)

1. D   2. E   3. F   4. C   5. B

6. A   7. I   8. J   9. G   10. H   11.–13. Sentences will vary.

Exercise B: Sorting (pages 50–51)

1.CIVI	**2. ORD**	**3. THERM**	**4. METER**	**5. STRUCT**	**6. TRACT**
civil	ordinarily	thermal	diameter	structure	contraction
civility	coordinate	thermometer	geometry	construction	extract
civics		thermostat	symmetrical	destructive	retraction
uncivilized			metronome	reconstruct	retract
civilian			perimeter		protractor

Answers will vary regarding the words that students add to the lists.

A. building   B. heat   C. being a citizen, a part of a city

D. *meter*   E. "heat" and "measurement"

Exercise C: Vocabulary from Your Textbook (page 51)

1. thermometer

2. contraction

3. civics

4. metronome

5. diameter, perimeter, protractor, geometry

Exercise D: Rhyming Riddles (page 52)

1. B   2. C   3. D   4. A   5. E

Exercise E: Writing and Discussion Activities (pages 52–53)

Answers will vary.

LESSON 13: CRACKING APART (PAGES 54–57)

Key Words

abrupt	fractional	fragility	interruption
disrupt	fracture	fragment	rupture

INTRODUCE LESSON 13

(page 54) Introduce Lesson 13 orally by having students read the title "Cracking Apart" and the two featured roots *frac/frag,* meaning "break," and *rupt,* meaning "burst."

Ask students for examples of things that break in contrast to things that burst. (Examples: A balloon bursts or pops; it does not break. The point of a lead pencil breaks; it does not burst. However, point out that in some cases the terms can be inter-changeable. A football player can *break* through or *burst* through a line of opponents.)

PREVIEW FAMILIAR WORDS

(pages 54, 55) *fraction, fragile, erupt, interrupt*

Activity 1: *frac/frag*

Display the familiar words *fraction* and *fragile.* Read them orally and then chorally with the class. Underline the root *frac* or *frag* in each one.

Ask students the following questions:

Hold up a cracker. Graham crackers that can be easily broken apart along the indenta-tion are ideal. Break the cracker in half, and hold up one half. Ask: How much of the cracker have I broken off? (half). How do you write that as a fraction? (1/2)

Name some things that are fragile, easily shattered or broken. (window panes, light-bulbs, water glasses) Tell about a time that you *broke* something that was fragile. (Stories will vary.)

Ask: What is the shared meaning for the root *frac/frag* in the words *fraction* and *fragile?* (break)

Activity 2: *rupt*

Display the familiar words *erupt* and *interrupt.* Read them orally and then chorally with the class. Underline the root *rupt* in each one.

Ask students the following questions:

How does the word *interrupt* relate to the idea of burst? (When people interrupt they *burst* into the conversation.) When a volcano erupts, what is happening? (Lava and ash and fire *burst* out from the top of the volcano.)

Ask: What is the shared meaning for the root *rupt* in *erupt* and *interrupt*? (burst)

PRESENT KEY WORDS

Display the key words. Read them orally and then chorally with the class.

Have students underline the root in each key word in the box on page 54; then have them check to be sure that their words look like this.

ab<u>rupt</u>	<u>frac</u>tional	<u>frag</u>ility	inter<u>rupt</u>ion
dis<u>rupt</u>	<u>frac</u>ture	<u>frag</u>ment	<u>rupt</u>ure

Ask students the following questions:

Which words begin with a root? (*fractional, fracture, fragility, fragment, rupture*)

In which words does the root *not* appear at the beginning? (*abrupt, disrupt, interruption*)

The words *abrupt, disrupt,* and *interruption* start with the prefixes *ab-, dis-,* and *inter-.*

You met the prefix *inter-* in a preceding lesson. What does it mean? (between) So, what is an interruption? (a *bursting* in, on something that is already in progress)

Could constant interruptions *disrupt* our class? (Yes, interruptions lead to *disruption*, which leads to disorder.)

The prefix *ab-* often means "away from." So the meaning clues for *abrupt* lead you to think "bursting away from." If you hear that a person made an "*abrupt* departure," do you think that the person lingered over good-bys or rushed out the door? (rushed out the door)

As students complete the "Using Root Clues" section, encourage them to use the meanings of the roots to find the correct answer. Have them match the columns <u>before</u> they study the complete definitions of the words.

Dictate answers so that students can check themselves.

(page 54) 1. B   2. A   3. D   4. C

Present each key word, paying attention to pronunciation, part of speech, definition with context sentence, and other parts of the listing as applicable (additional derivation, related word form, illustration).

In this lesson the schwa (ə) occurs in every word, in accented as well as unaccented syllables, so these listings offer a good opportunity to review the schwa and the other diacritical marks from the inside front cover.

The word *fragility* also offers a good opportunity for review, since the *-ity* suffix was presented in Lesson 9. What key word on page 37 ends in that suffix? (*civility*) What part of speech are *fragility, civility,* and most other words that end in that suffix? (nouns)

GUIDE ORAL PRACTICE
Activity 1: Connections and Examples

Explain that sometimes there is a strong literal connection between the meaning of a word and the meaning of its root. The connection is very easy to see. Other times the connection is not as literal, so it is not as easy to see.

Which word—*rupture* or *abrupt*—has the more literal connection with the "bursting" meaning of the root *rupt*? (*Rupture* has the more literal connection; a ruptured appendix has actually *burst* inside a person. The adjective *abrupt* means "sudden" or "unexpected," and bursting is usually sudden or unexpected, but its connection with the root *rupt* is not as literal.)

Which word—*fractional* or *fracture*—has a more literal connection with the "breaking" meaning of the root *frac*? (*Fracture* has a more literal connection since a fracture is a break. A fractional part may be "broken" away from the whole, but the connection with *frac* is not as literal since a fraction does not immediately bring to mind the idea of breaking.)

Activity 2: Draw, Display, Discuss

Ask: Where or when have you seen a fragment? (Probably at home in the kitchen when someone dropped a plate or a glass, and it broke into little pieces. Fragments of china, plastic, or glass may have scattered all over the floor.)

Display two cups, one that is unbreakable like a baby's cup and the other that is fragile. Why are cups for babies made of unbreakable material? (Babies and toddlers drop their cups, and even throw them, when they are just learning how to handle tableware.)

On the board, draw a box with the mailing label, "Fragile. Handle with Care." Have students draw three items that they think might be packed in the box. (Examples: fine tableware, china dolls, holiday ornaments, mirrors)

ASSIGN WRITTEN EXERCISES
Exercise A: Synonyms (page 56)

1. d   2. b   3. a   4. d   5. c

Exercise B: Meaning in Context (page 56)

1. fragments   2. fragility   3. interruption   4. fractional   5. disrupt

Exercise C: Extend Your Vocabulary (pages 56–57)

complete word + *-ment*	root + *-ment*
punishment	monument
improvement	document
government	ornament
amusement	instrument
management	
development	

1. nouns
2. verbs
3. It changes a verb into a noun.
4. second column
5. nouns

Reproducible Worksheet: Lesson 13 (page 72 in this book)

LESSON 14: PLACING THE FOUNDATION (PAGES 58–61)

Key Words

basement	bass	dispose	position
basis	composition	exposure	positive

INTRODUCE LESSON 14

(page 58) Introduce Lesson 14 orally by having students read the title "Placing the Foundation" and the two featured roots *bas,* meaning "foundation, low part," and *pos,* meaning "placement."

PREVIEW FAMILIAR WORDS

(pages 58, 59) *base, baseboard, basic, pose, post, poster, posture*

Activity 1: *bas*

Display the familiar words *base, baseboard, basic.* Read them orally and then chorally with the class. Underline the root *bas* in each one.

Ask students the following questions:

Where is the base of a statue? (at the bottom, the *low*est part. The base or pedestal supports the statue.)

Where are the baseboards in a room? (*low,* bordering the floor at each wall)

What *basic* information do you give when you write your address? (the number and name of your street, your apartment number (if applicable), your city, state, and zip code)

What do we mean when we say this information is "basic"? (It is the *lowest* limit of what information the post office must have to be able to deliver the mail.)

Ask: What are the shared meanings for the root *bas* in the words *base, baseboard, basic*? (low, foundation)

Activity 2: *pos*

Display the familiar words *pose, post, poster, posture.* Read them orally and then chorally with the class. Underline *pos* in each one.

Ask students to assume *poses* to suggest the following:

a weightlifter, a sprinter about to start a race, a nurse about to give a shot, and so on. Have other students critique the poses and make suggestions when necessary. What connection is there between the meaning of the word *pose* and the root *pos*? (*Pos* means placement or position. A *pose* is taking a fixed position.)

Ask students to demonstrate good posture while standing, sitting, walking. Then, ask them to demonstrate poor posture while doing the same actions. Have them describe what the *placement* of the shoulders should be for good posture. Why is good posture important? (shoulders back; for the bones to align)

What is a poster for? (to give information about some event, idea, and so on) Where do you *place* posters? (in locations where the most people will see them)

Why do you think we usually use the word *post* when we are talking about posters or notices of some kind? (We are positioning things in the best *place*.)

Ask: What is the shared meaning for the root *pos* in *pose, post, poster, posture*? (place or put)

PRESENT KEY WORDS

Display the key words. Read them orally and then chorally with the class.

Have students underline the root in each key word in the box on page 58; then have them check to be sure that their words look like this.

| basement | bass | dispose | position |
| basis | composition | exposure | positive |

Which key words begin with a root? (*basement, basis, bass, position, positive*)

Which three of the eight featured words do *not* begin with a root? (*composition, dispose, exposure*)

You met the prefix *ex-* in a previous lesson. What does *ex-* mean? (out)

Using this information, what do the think *exposure* might mean? (some form of "putting out," putting outside, putting out for all to see)

As students complete the "Using Root Clues" section, encourage them to use the meanings of the roots to find the correct answer. Have them match the columns <u>before</u> they study the complete definitions of the words.

Dictate answers so that students can check themselves.

(page 58) 1. D   2. C   3. A   4. B

Present each key word, paying attention to pronunciation, part of speech, definition with context sentence, and other parts of the listing as applicable (additional derivation, related word form, illustration).

In this lesson, all five of the words with the root *pos* have multiple meanings.

Which meaning of *composition* is more familiar to you? (probably the first one, since writing compositions is done frequently in school)

Which meaning of *dispose* is shown in the illustration? (the first)

Which meaning of *exposure* is connected with extreme heat or cold? (the first)

There are three definitions of *position*. Which would relate to a debate? (the third)

Which definition of *positive* is the opposite of *negative?* (the second)

GUIDE ORAL PRACTICE
Activity 1: Connections and Examples

How are the words *basement* and *bass* connected with the "low" meaning of the root *bas?* (The basement is the *low*est floor of a building. The boys in the bass section of a chorus have the *low*est voices.)

How is the word *basis* connected with the "foundation" meaning of the root *bas?* (The basis of a judgment is the foundation of evidence on which it rests.)

Explain that sometimes there is a strong literal connection between the meaning of a word and the meaning of its root. The connection is very easy to see. Other times the connection is not as literal, so it is not as easy to see.

Which word—*positive* or *position*—has a stronger connection with the "placement" meaning of the root *pos?* (*Position* has the stronger connection since the definition of position is "placement." *Positive* has a connection, since it can mean "sure about where you stand," but the connection is not as strong.)

Activity 2: Draw, Display, Discuss

Show or explain how you can *dispose*, or get rid, of something. (A student might throw a paper in the wastebasket. Another student might suggest disposing of clothes that you've outgrown by giving them to others, such as younger relatives or to a charity.) What does a garbage disposal do? (It grinds up and gets rid of kitchen food waste.)

Make a drawing showing a situation where people could suffer from exposure. (Situations will vary but might show people exposed to sun, water, cold, and so on.)

ASSIGN WRITTEN EXERCISES
Exercise A: Synonyms (page 60)

1. a   2. b   3. d   4. b   5. c

Exercise B: Meaning in Context (page 61)

1. basement   2. position   3. positive   4. dispose

Exercise C: Extend Your Vocabulary (page 61)

1. signature   2. mixture   3. pleasure   4. fracture   5. rupture

Reproducible Worksheet: Lesson 14 (page 73 in this book)

LESSON 15: CONNECTING WITH PREFIXES (PAGES 62–66)

> ## Key Words
>
> committee   conjunction   reaction   reflect
>
> communicate   converse   reelect   relate

INTRODUCE LESSON 15

(page 62) Introduce Lesson 15 orally by having students read the title "Connecting with Prefixes" and the two featured prefixes *com-/con-*, meaning "together; with" and *re-*, meaning "again; back."

Point out that prefixes can have more than one meaning. Consider the word *retract*; what does it mean? (It means "to take or pull something *back*.") Consider the word *reread*; what does it mean? (It means "to read *again*.")

Sometimes the two meanings of *re-* overlap: to *review* is "to look *back* and study *again*."

PREVIEW FAMILIAR WORDS

(pages 63, 64) *combine, commotion, compare, conductor, congress, connection*

rearrange, recall, repeat, return review, rewrite

Activity 1: *com-/con-*

Display the familiar words *combine, commotion, compare, conductor, congress, connection*. Read them orally and then chorally with the class. Underline the prefix *com-* or *con-* in each one.

Ask students the following questions:

What does the *conductor* of a band or orchestra do? (This person is the one who keeps all the musicians playing in time *together* by waving a baton.)

What is the "with" *connection* for the familiar words *compare* and *combine*? (You compare one thing *with* another, and you combine one thing *with* another.)

What are some places that usually have a lot of *commotion*? (Answers will vary but may include a train or bus station, an airport just before a scheduled departure, backstage before a play, locker rooms after a winning game, and so on.) What connection does *commotion* have with the "together; with" meaning of the *com-* prefix? (A commotion is the movement of many people or animals together.)

What is Congress? (the meeting together of the lawmakers from all the states)

Ask: What is the shared meaning for the prefix *com-/con-* in the familiar words *combine, commotion, compare, conductor, congress, connection*? (with, together)

Activity 2: *re-*

Display the familiar words *rearrange, recall, repeat, return, review, rewrite.* Read them orally and then chorally with the class. Underline *re-* in each one.

Ask students the following questions:

When you ask me to repeat a statement, what do you want me to do? (say it *again*)

Which familiar word describes what you do when you go *back* home because you have forgotten something? (return)

What do you recall about your last birthday party? (Memories will vary, but point out to students that they are bringing the birthday party *back* to mind and are thinking about it *again* as they recall.)

Discuss the "back; again" connection for the familiar words *rearrange, review,* and *rewrite.* (Examples: When you rearrange the clothes in your closet, you have to go *back* to the closet, take out some hangers, and put them in *again* in different positions. When you review a chapter, you look *back* at the pages and read them *again.* When you rewrite a paper, you sometimes have to go *back* and start all over *again.*)

Ask: What is the shared meaning for the root *re-* in *rearrange, recall, repeat, return, review, rewrite?* (back and/or again)

PRESENT KEY WORDS

Display the key words. Read them orally and then chorally with the class.

Have students underline the prefix in each key word in the box on page 62; then have them check to be sure that the words look like this.

committee	conjunction	reaction	reflect
communicate	converse	reelect	relate

There are eight key words in Lesson 15. How many begin with a prefix? (all eight)

The roots, as well as the prefixes, of some key words give you clues to meaning. Also, you may find that you are familiar with a base word to which one of the prefixes has been added.

What part of speech is the word *reelect?* (a verb) If you take off the prefix *re-,* what base word is left? (*elect*) What part of speech is the base word? (a verb also) Who was elected president in our last election? Can that person be reelected? Why or why not?

What part of speech is the word *reaction?* (a noun) If you take off the prefix *re-,* what is left? (the word *action*) What part of speech is the base word? (a noun also) If someone smiles at you, what is your natural reaction? (to smile back at that person)

As students complete the "Using Prefix Clues" section, encourage them to use the meanings of the prefixes to find the correct answer. Have them match the columns before they study the complete definitions of the words.

Dictate answers so that students can check themselves.

(page 62) 1. B   2. C   3. A   4. D

Present each key word, paying attention to pronunciation, part of speech, definition with context sentence, and other parts of the listing as applicable (additional derivation, related word form, illustration).

On page 63, ask: What is the derivation of the root of the word *conjunction*? (the Latin *jungere* meaning "to join") What other words can you think of that are derived from that root? (Examples: *junction* and *juncture*, which can both be defined as places where two roads join)

On page 64, how many definitions do you see for the word *reflect*? (two) What related form of the word appears at the end of the listing? (reflection) Compose two definitions of *reflection* that parallel the two definitions of *reflect*. (1. an image thrown back by light, and 2. the act of thinking back about or considering carefully)

GUIDE ORAL PRACTICE

Activity 1: Connections and Examples

The key words *communicate, converse,* and *relate* can be called synonyms, since they are similar in meaning, but not exactly alike. To some degree, all three of these verbs are connected with talking.

Which one includes not only talking but also writing, broadcasting, sign language, and electronic transmission of messages? (*communicate*)

Which one makes you think of at least two people talking back and forth? (*converse*)

Which word could refer to the telling of a story by one person? (*relate*)

Perhaps you know still another definition connected with *relate*. What do you call the people who are *related* to you? (relatives) What are some categories of relatives? (uncles, aunts, cousins, grandparents)

What word do you make if you subtract the prefix *con-* from *conjunction*? (*junction*)

What is the "junction point" of two roads? (the place where they join or meet)

Parts of speech have functions; for example, the function of a noun is "to name." What is the function of a conjunction? (to join)

Activity 2: Draw, Display, Discuss

Tell students to draw stick figures to represent a committee. How many did each student draw? (Compare the numbers they showed—probably more than two and less than ten.) Discuss sizes and purposes of committees.

Ask: How many coordinating conjunctions, or joining words, can we list? (*and, but, or, nor*)

ASSIGN WRITTEN EXERCISES

Exercise A: Synonyms (page 65)

1. d   2. b   3. d   4. a   5. c

Exercise B: Meaning in Context (page 65)

1. Committee   2. related   3. conversed   4. reaction   5. reelected

Exercise C: Extend Your Vocabulary (pages 65–66)

COM-	CON-	OTHER
community	concert	collision
companion	congruent	collage
company	connection	coordinate
		correspondence

1. concert
2. collage
3. collision
4. connection
5. companion
6. together, with

Reproducible Worksheet: Lesson 15 (page 74 in this book)

LESSON 16: REVIEWING LESSONS 13–15 (PAGES 67–71)

Before your students do the written review exercises in the book, conduct an oral review of the meanings of the featured roots and prefixes, the word parts from the Exercise Cs, and the key vocabulary from Lessons 13, 14, and 15.

DISCUSS

Use these kinds of questions to challenge students.

What is the connection in meaning between the words *basement* and *basis*? (They both have the *bas* root, which can mean "foundation"; the *basement* is built on the *foundation* of a house, and the *basis* of a position is its *foundation*.) Lesson 14

Using the meanings of the prefixes and roots, explain the difference between *composing* and *exposing*. (The words share the root *pos*, meaning "put; place." *Com-* with *pos* gives the meaning of "putting or placing together." *Ex-* and *pos* give the meaning of "putting or placing out.") Lesson 14

How do the meanings "back" and "again" overlap in the word *reflect*? (When you think *back* or reflect about something, you are thinking about it *again*.) Lesson 15

What is a conjunction? (a joining together.) What part of the word *conjunction* gives you the "together" clue? (the prefix *con-*) Lesson 15

The words *fracture* and *rupture* can be used as two different parts of speech. Which two? (noun and verb) Lesson 13

REINFORCE

What part of speech do you associate with the suffixes *-ure* and *-ment*? (noun) Lessons 13, 14

Use the noun *rupture* in a sentence. (Sentences will vary.) Lessons 13, 14

Use the noun *fragment* in a sentence. (Sentences will vary.) Lesson 13

The *com-/con-* prefix can be spelled in other ways, such as *co-*, *col-*, and *cor-*. Think of words that have these prefixes, and use them in sentences that show the "with, together" meaning. Check your dictionary if you need help. (Sentences will vary.) Lesson 15

EXPLORE

When students would benefit from a more in-depth exploration of a particular word, the additional word-learning strategies at the beginning of this book (pages vi–viii) can be helpful.

GUIDE ORAL PRACTICE
Activity 1: Definition Challenge

Give each student a card (3" by 5" or 5" by 7"). Assign each student one of the twenty-four words from the box at the top of page 68 in the student book. Have the student copy the complete definition of that word on the card. Line up the class in two teams, facing each other.

The first student on Team A reads a definition. The first student on Team B can earn two points by coming up with the word that fits the definition. If the answer is incorrect, Team B may still earn one point if another member can come up with the word.

The teams take turns until all the definitions have been read. The team with the most points wins.

Activity 2: Charades (sorting by parts of speech)

Hand each student another blank card (3" by 5" or 5" by 7"). Again assign to each student one of the twenty-four words, but make sure it is a different one from the word the student had for Activity 1. The student will copy the new word and its full definition from the book.

Write these categories on the board: nouns, verbs, adjectives, nouns and verbs. Tell students to sort themselves into these four groups, according to the part of speech of their assigned words. Their groupings should look like this:

Nouns	Verbs	Adjectives	Nouns and Verbs
basement	communicate	abrupt	fracture
basis	converse	bass	rupture
committee	dispose	fractional	
composition	disrupt	positive	
conjunction	reelect		
exposure	reflect		
fragility	relate		
fragment			
interruption			
position			
reaction			

Let the two students holding the words *fracture* and *rupture* move to the group with adjectives; then split the group of nouns in half.

Tell each group to select two of their words to act out, as in charades. Allow a little time for each group to plan what they will do. All of the group's words should stay on display while the acting is taking place. The other students have to guess which word is being portrayed.

Activity 3: Charades (sorting by syllables)

Have each student give his or her word card from the previous activity to another student. Tell students to sort themselves into new groups, according to the number of syllables in their word. Then, have each group line up in alphabetical order, while holding up their cards. Their groupings should look like this:

One	Two	Three	Four
bass	abrupt	committee	communicate
	basement	conjunction	composition
	basis	exposure	fragility
	converse	fractional	interruption
	dispose	position	
	disrupt	positive	
	fracture	reaction	
	fragment	reelect	
	reflect		
	relate		
	rupture		

Arrange students in two groups. Have the student with the one-syllable word *bass* join the two-syllable group and have students with three- and four-syllable words work together. Proceed as above, with each group planning charades for two words.

ASSIGN WRITTEN EXERCISES

Exercise A: Matching (page 67)

1. C   2. A   3. D   4. B   5. F   6. E   7.–11. Sentences will vary.

Exercise B: Sorting (pages 68–69)

1. FRAC/FRAG	2. RUPT	3. POS
fracture	abrupt	positive
fragility	disrupt	position
fragment	rupture	*composition*
fractional	interruption	exposure
		dispose

4. BAS	**5. COM-/CON-**	**6. RE-**
basement	committee	reflect
basis	*composition*	reelect
bass	communicate	relate
	converse	reaction
	conjunction	

Answers will vary regarding the words that students add to the lists.

A. 5   B. 6   C. *composition*   D. "bursting" and "the result of"

Exercise C: Vocabulary from Your Textbooks (page 69)

1. bass   2. fracture   3. reelect   4. fragility   5. fractional

Exercise D: Rhyming Riddles (page 70)

1. E   2. C   3. B   4. F   5. D   6. A

Exercise E: Writing or Discussion Activities (pages 70–71)

Answers will vary.

Lesson 1 Word Activity Master: Going in Circles (*circ* and *cycl*)

Name _____ Date _____

Synonym Tic-tac-toe

For each numbered word, find a row of synonyms and draw a line through it. The row can be horizontal, vertical, or diagonal. Remember that synonyms are similar in meaning, but <u>not</u> exactly alike.

1. CIRCULATE		
move	sleep	push
flow	read	study
pass	jump	operate

2. WINDSTORM		
snow	weather	seashore
cyclone	tornado	hurricane
newscast	business	recess

3. CIRCUIT		
route	picture	headline
star	path	school
dress	sign	course

4. CIRCULAR		
round	curved	encircling
open	quick	rectangular
smart	quiet	written

Matching

Match each word in the first column with an example in the second column.

5. ____ cycle

6. ____ semicircle

7. ____ cyclone

8. ____ recycling

A. half of a pie

B. spring, summer, fall, winter

C. wearing a shirt someone else has outgrown

D. the storm in *The Wizard of Oz*

Sentences

Write a sentence or two to answer the following questions. Use the underlined word in your answer.

9. When is the sun in the shape of a <u>semicircle</u>? _____

_____

10. How could a sharp nail damage a <u>unicycle</u>? _____

_____

Lesson 2 Word Activity Master: Balancing Evenly (*equ* and *pend*)

Name _____ Date _____

Where

Match each item with the place where you would be likely to find it.

1. ____ equator
2. ____ pendulum
3. ____ an equilateral shape
4. ____ dependent students
5. ____ equality of length
6. ____ four puppies

A. in a store that sells carpet squares
B. on a globe
C. in a nursery-school classroom
D. in a box of new crayons
E. in a litter of quadruplets
F. in a clock

Names of Shapes

Answer the following questions with the name of the shape described.

7. What is the name of an equilateral quadrilateral? _____

8. What is the name of a quadrilateral with four right angles, but that is not equilateral?

_____

9. What is the name of a half-circle? _____

10. What is the name of a three-sided figure on which the sides are equal in length?

_____   _____

True or False

Write *true* or *false* after each of these sentences, according to the meaning of the word in italics. Be prepared to explain your answers orally.

1. Colorado is *equidistant* from the East and West coasts. _____

2. With a measuring cup, a cook can *equate* the amounts of milk and water. _____

3. The *equator* passes through southern Florida and California. _____

4. After the jury reached its verdict, its decision was *pending*. _____

5. A car's ability to stop quickly is *dependent* upon good brakes. _____

6. In football, a *lateral* pass is thrown straight ahead. _____

Lesson 3 Word Activity Master: Moving Across and Between (*trans* and *inter*)

Name _____ Date _____

Synonym Tic-tac-toe

For each numbered word, find a row of synonyms and draw a line through it. The row can be horizontal, vertical, or diagonal. Remember that synonyms are similar in meaning, but <u>not</u> exactly alike.

1. TRANSACT		
read	suffer	decorate
dash	steal	insult
do	conduct	perform

2. INTERMITTENT		
steady	silent	off-and-on
loud	endless	irregular
dark	noisy	variable

3. INTERFERE		
meddle	eat	agree
laugh	intervene	dance
produce	use	hinder

4. TRANSMIT		
stop	study	send
think	deliver	interest
convey	plant	wiggle

Matching

Match the word in the first column with the object or activity in the second column that is related to it.

5. ____ intersection

6. ____ transfer

7. ____ transfusion

8. ____ intermittent

A. a doctor

B. red, yellow, and green lights

C. an activated burglar alarm

D. changing buses

Sentences

Write a sentence or two to answer the following questions. Use the underlined word in your answer.

9. How long is the <u>interval</u> between the end of your school day and your arrival at home?

_____

_____

10. Describe an <u>interactive</u> game you enjoy playing. _____

_____

_____

Lesson 5 Word Activity Master: Looking at Our Planet (*aqua* and *terr*)

Name _____ Date _____

Which
Write the correct word to answer each question.

1. Which is larger—a terrace or a territory? _____

2. Which describes an underground passageway—subterranean or submarine? _____

3. Which is connected with farming—marina or aquaculture? _____

4. Which live in water—aquatic creatures or subterranean creatures? _____

5. Which continent borders the Mediterranean Sea—Africa or Australia? _____

What
Use the following words to answer the questions below.

mariner   **territory**   **marine**   **marina**   **terrace**

6. What types of plants live underwater? _____

7. What is a synonym of the word *patio*? _____

8. What do you call a place where many boats are docked? _____

9. What is a synonym of the word *sailor*? _____

10. What do you call a large region of land? _____

Where
Match each item with the place where you can find it.

11. ____ tadpoles   A. in an aquamarine sea

12. ____ blue-green waves   B. at one end of the Mediterranean Sea

13. ____ Strait of Gibraltar   C. unpaved terrain

14. ____ rough and bumpy travel   D. in an aquatic environment

Sentence

15. Use three key words in a sentence describing a bumpy footpath through a colorful underground cave.

_____

Lesson 6 Word Activity Master: Exploring Distant Places (*astr* and *tele*)

Name _____ Date _____

Cross-Synonym Puzzle

Fill in the blanks with synonyms of the vertical word *astronomical* in this cross-synonym puzzle. The top one is done for you.

gigantic   immense   colossal   tremendous   enormous   vast

```
V A S T
  S
  T □ □ □ □ □ □
  R
□ □ □ □ □ O □ □
  N
  O
□ □ M □ □ □
  I
□ □ □ □ □ □ C
  A
□ □ □ □ L □ □ □
```

Which

Answer each question and then explain your answer.

1. Which word was created first—*telecast* or *television?* _____

_____

2. Which word is older—*teleconference* or *telephone?* _____

_____

3. Which word is more recent—*telegraph* or *telemarketing?* _____

_____

4. Which job has existed longer—that of an *astronaut* or that of a *mariner?* _____

_____

5. Which tool will a student of astronomy use most: a telescope, a microscope, or a telegraph?

_____

Lesson 7 Word Activity Master: Changing Meaning with Prefixes (*in-* and *semi-*

Name _____ Date _____

Synonym Tic-tac-toe

For each numbered word, find a row of synonyms and draw a line through it. The row can be horizontal, vertical, or diagonal. Remember that synonyms are similar in meaning, but <u>not</u> exactly alike.

1. INACTIVE		
quick	possible	lovely
idle	motionless	passive
damp	semiprecious	truthful

2. INSIGNIFICANT		
healthy	young	unimportant
golden	trivial	separate
nonessential	united	semiannual

3. SEMICONSCIOUS		
powerful	dazed	upset
surprised	drowsy	hungry
semiformal	insensible	private

4. INSOMNIA		
wakefulness	transaction	semicolon
government	restlessness	astronomy
telemarketing	aquaculture	sleeplessness

Antonyms

Add a prefix that means "not" to each word to make its antonym (opposite).

5. formal _____

6. active _____

7. practical _____

8. regular _____

Matching

You learned the words *dependent, circular, aquatic,* and *equality* in previous lessons. Use your knowledge of the prefixes *in-* and *semi-*, which have been added to these words, to match the new words with their meanings.

9. ____ independent

A. living part of the time in water

10. ____ semicircular

B. unfairness

11. ____ semiaquatic

C. in a half circle

12. ____ inequality

D. not relying on or controlled by others

68

Lesson 9 Word Activity Master: Creating Order (*civi* and *ord*)

Name _____ Date _____

Which
Choose one of the following words to answer the questions below.

civility   civilian   civilize   uncivilized

1. Which word has a negative prefix? _____

2. Which word is a verb? _____

3. Which word is a noun that names a person? _____

4. Which word is a noun related to the adjective *civil?* _____

5. Write a sentence in which you use both nouns. _____

_____

Synonym Tic-tac-toe
For each numbered word, find a row of synonyms and draw a line through it. The row can be horizontal, vertical, or diagonal. Remember that synonyms are similar in meaning, but <u>not</u> exactly alike.

6. ORDINARILY		
rapidly	hurriedly	easily
wisely	equally	immediately
usually	generally	commonly

7. EXTRAORDINARY		
remarkable	orderly	short
steady	unusual	lengthy
forgettable	circular	amazing

8. CIVILITY		
difference	imagination	activity
liberty	possibility	friendship
courtesy	politeness	mannerliness

9. UNCIVILIZED		
wild	broad	patient
primitive	private	complete
disorderly	hidden	scientific

Sentence
Write a sentence or two to answer the following question. Use the underlined word in your answer.

10. How do you *coordinate* all the activities on your schedule to allow enough time for homework and entertainment?

_____

Lesson 10 Word Activity Master: Measuring in Math and Science (*metr/meter* and *therm*)

Name _____ Date _____

Measuring

Choose one of the following words to answer each question below.

kilometer   metronome   geometry   millimeter   meter

1. Which measurement is a little longer than a yard? _____

2. Which is one one-thousandth of a meter? _____

3. In which subject do you learn to measure shapes? _____

4. Which is equal to about 5/8 of a mile? _____

5. Which ticks to measure time for musicians? _____

Symmetry

6. If you fold certain letters in half along a vertical line, they are the same on both sides. Decide which of the following letters are symmetrical when folded in that way and circle them.

   A   F   H   M   O   P   R   V   X

7. Are the halves of a circle symmetrical?   Yes   No

8. Are the halves of a square symmetrical?   Yes   No

9. Are the halves of an equilateral triangle symmetrical?   Yes   No

10. Fold a sheet of paper and cut out a symmetrical figure. (Examples: a tree, a person, a house.) Explain why the figure is symmetrical.

_____

Matching

Match the words in the first column with an appropriate purpose in the second column.

11. ____ perimeter measure   A. to check the temperature inside the turkey as it bakes

12. ____ thermometer   B. to figure out how much fencing to buy to enclose the yard

13. ____ thermostat   C. to help musicians play at the same speed

14. ____ metronome   D. to make sure the house does not get too cold at night

Lesson 11 Word Activity Master: Pulling Together (*struct* and *tract*)

Name _____ Date _____

Meaningful Parts

Inside the word *reconstruction*, there are a number of meaningful parts, some of which are whole words.

1. Which part (a word) means "to build"? _____

2. Which part (a prefix) means "again"? _____

3. Which part (a word) means "to build again"? _____

4. Which part (a word) means "the act of putting together"? _____

Prefixes with the Root *tract*

These prefixes can be added to the root *tract* to make words: *ex-, re-, sub-, at-*. Add one of the prefixes to *tract* to make the word for each of these meanings.

5. to pull back   _____

6. to pull out   _____

7. to pull away or down _____

8. to pull toward   _____

Sentences

Write a sentence or two to answer the following questions. Use the underlined words in your answers.

9. Why does a <u>construction</u> worker wear a hard hat? _____

_____

10. In what way can a storm be <u>destructive</u> to a <u>structure</u>? _____

_____

11. What does the apostrophe stand for in a <u>contraction</u>? _____

_____

12. When might a doctor prescribe <u>traction</u>? _____

_____

Lesson 13 Word Activity Master: Cracking Apart (*frac/frag* and *rupt*)

Name _____ Date _____

Clues

Beside each clue, write either *fracture* or *rupture*.

1. a cracked rib

       _____

2. a garden hose spurting water from a small hole

       _____

3. a broken bone that needs a cast

       _____

4. a crack in a stone statue

       _____

Synonym Tic-tac-toe

For each numbered word, find a row of synonyms and draw a line through it. The row can be horizontal, vertical, or diagonal. Remember that synonyms are similar in meaning, but <u>not</u> exactly alike.

5. ABRUPTLY		
carefully	easily	suddenly
slowly	partly	unexpectedly
warmly	bravely	instantly

6. DISRUPT		
buy	bathe	irritate
treat	interrupt	cheer
disturb	purchase	comfort

7. FRAGILITY		
brittleness	delicacy	weakness
wisdom	strength	civility
health	possibility	journey

8. AMUSEMENT		
entertainment	interaction	torment
fragment	recreation	punishment
monument	civilization	merriment

Sentences

Write a sentence or two to respond to the directions. Use the underlined words in what you write.

9. Explain why <u>fragments</u> are bound to be <u>fractional</u> parts. _____

_____

10. Compose a sentence that contains two nouns that end in the suffix *-ment*. _____

_____

Lesson 14 Word Activity Master: Placing the Foundation (*bas* and *pos*)

Name _____ Date _____

Matching
Match each item with the place where you are likely to find it.

1. ___ basement   A. in a chorus

2. ___ disposal   B. at the end of a letter

3. ___ signature   C. below the first floor

4. ___ bass section   D. in the pile with gold stars

5. ___ best compositions   E. under the kitchen sink

Antonyms
Use these words to fill in the lines below with antonyms (opposites).

       positive   basement   exposed   mixture   bass

6. attic   _____

7. negative   _____

8. soprano   _____

9. hidden   _____

10. separation   _____

True or False
Write *true* or *false* after each of these sentences, according to the meaning of the word in italics. Be prepared to explain your answers orally.

11. Judges make decisions on the *basis* of the evidence. _____

12. *Positive* comments about your work will make you angry. _____

13. The *position* of senator is an elected office. _____

14. *Exposure* to secondhand smoke is harmless. _____

15. The *composition* of granite includes feathers, mica, and shells. _____

Name _____ Date _____

Synonym Tic-tac-toe

For each numbered word, find a row of synonyms and draw a line through it. The row can be horizontal, vertical, or diagonal. Remember that synonyms are similar in meaning, but not exactly alike.

1. REFLECT		
carry	arrange	share
think	consider	ponder
kick	overtake	reelect

2. RELATE		
begin	tell	wave
renew	report	dance
elect	speak	desire

3. COMMITTEE		
group	musicians	reaction
civilian	council	conjunction
equality	protractor	board

4. COMMUNICATE		
measure	ride	explain
include	talk	drink
inform	leave	pack

Other Synonyms

Note that the synonyms above for *relate* and *communicate* are similar.

In each line below, circle two other words that belong to the same family of synonyms for "relate" and "communicate."

5. say, run, notify, continue, depend

6. declare, jump, extract, swing, announce

7. return, disclose, convey, shatter, renew

8. converse, chase, overtake, reveal, think

Sentences

Write a sentence or two when you give your answers.

9. Which two presidents do you think most deserved to be *reelected* for a second term? Why?

_____

_____

10. Compose a sentence in which you use two *conjunctions*. Then underline them.

_____

_____

LESSON 1 WORD ACTIVITY MASTER ANSWERS (SEE PAGE 63)

Synonym Tic-tac-toe

1. CIRCULATE: (first column) move, flow, pass

2. WINDSTORM: (second row) cyclone, tornado, hurricane

3. CIRCUIT: (diagonal, left top to right bottom) route, path, course

4. CIRCULAR: (first row) round, curved, encircling

Matching

5. B   6. A   7. D   8. C

Sentences

9. The sun may appear as a <u>semicircle</u> at dawn as it rises above the horizon or at dusk as it drops below the horizon.

10. A sharp nail could puncture the wheel of a <u>unicycle</u> and cause a flat tire.

LESSON 2 WORD ACTIVITY MASTER ANSWERS (SEE PAGE 64)

Where

1. B   2. F   3. A   4. C   5. D   6. E

Names of Shapes

7. square   8. rectangle   9. semicircle   10. equilateral triangle

True or False

Since students are instructed to explain their answers orally in terms of the italicized words have them debate any differences among these answers.

1. False   4. False

2. True   5. True

3. False   6. False

LESSON 3 WORD ACTIVITY MASTER ANSWERS (SEE PAGE 65)

Synonym Tic-tac-toe

1. TRANSACT: (third row) do, conduct, perform

2. INTERMITTENT: (third column) off-and-on, irregular, variable

3. INTERFERE: (diagonal, left top to right bottom) meddle, intervene, hinder

4. TRANSMIT: (diagonal, left bottom to right top) convey, deliver, send

Matching

5. B   6. D   7. A   8. C

Sentences

9. Answers will vary. Example: The <u>interval</u> is less than half an hour since the school bus gets me home quickly.

10. Answers will vary. Example: I enjoy playing tennis. I hit the ball to my opponent who returns it to me. The more <u>interaction</u> between us, the more enjoyable the game.

LESSON 5 WORD ACTIVITY MASTER ANSWERS (SEE PAGE 66)
Which

1. territory   2. subterranean   3. aquaculture   4. aquatic   5. Africa

What

6. marine   7. terrace   8. marina   9. mariner   10. territory

Where

11. D   12. A   13. B   14. C

Sentence

15. Answers will vary. Example: We kicked aside <u>aquamarine</u> pebbles as we made our way over the rough <u>terrain</u> of the footpath in the <u>subterranean</u> cave.

LESSON 6 WORD ACTIVITY MASTER ANSWERS (SEE PAGE 67)
Cross-Synonym Puzzle

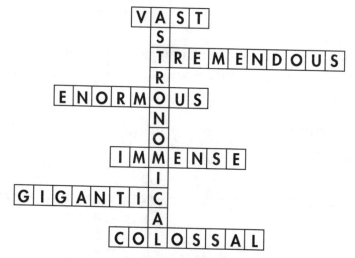

Which

1. Television. The instrument that carries the program must be invented first. The telecast or program would develop later.

2. Telephone. The telephone existed first and then people got the idea of finding a way for several people to talk with each other at the same time.

3. Telemarketing. The telegraph was invented in 1837, long before telephones became ubiquitous enough to think of using them to sell items.

4. Mariner. People have sailed the seas for thousands of years, but they have only begun sailing through space.

5. A telescope. A student of astronomy needs a tool for seeing objects that are far away rather than for magnifying objects that are near or for sending messages over long distances.

LESSON 7 WORD ACTIVITY MASTER ANSWERS (SEE PAGE 68)

Synonym Tic-tac-toe

1. INACTIVE: (second row) idle, motionless, passive

2. INSIGNIFICANT: (diagonal, top right to bottom left) unimportant, trivial, nonessential

3. SEMICONSCIOUS: (second column) dazed, drowsy, insensible

4. INSOMNIA: (diagonal, top left to bottom right) wakefulness, restlessness, sleeplessness

Antonyms

5. informal   6. inactive   7. impractical   8. irregular

Matching

9. D   10. C   11. A   12. B

LESSON 9 WORD ACTIVITY MASTER ANSWERS (SEE PAGE 69)

Which

1. uncivilized   2. civilize   3. civilian   4. civility

5. Sentences will vary. Example: It was hard for the <u>civilian</u> to behave with <u>civility</u> toward people he did not respect.

Synonym Tic-tac-toe

6. ORDINARILY: (bottom row) usually, generally, commonly

7. EXTRAORDINARY: (diagonal, left top to right bottom) remarkable, unusual, amazing

8. CIVILITY: (bottom row) courtesy, politeness, mannerliness

9. UNCIVILIZED: (first column) wild, primitive, disorderly

Sentences

10. Sentences will vary. Example: I make a schedule so that I can <u>coordinate</u> my regular activities, like dressing, eating, and going to school, with finishing homework and doing things for fun.

LESSON 10 WORD KEY MASTER ANSWERS (SEE PAGE 70)
Measuring

1. meter   2. millimeter   3. geometry   4. kilometer   5. metronome

Symmetry

6. A, H, M, O, V, X   7. Yes   8. Yes   9. Yes

10. The figure is symmetrical because it is the same on both sides of the fold.

Matching

11. B   12. A   13. D   14. C

LESSON 11 WORD ACTIVITY MASTER ANSWERS (SEE PAGE 71)
Meaningful Parts

1. construct   2. re-   3. reconstruct   4. construction

Prefixes with the Root *tract*

5. retract   6. extract   7. subtract   8. attract

Sentences

Sentences will vary, but here are some examples:

9. A *construction* worker wears a hard hat to protect his head from building materials that might fall on him.

10. A storm can be *destructive* to a *structure* like a house by blowing off its roof.

11. In a *contraction*, the apostrophe stands for the letter or letters that are left out.

12. A doctor might prescribe *traction* for a patient with a broken bone that needed to be pulled and held in position for healing.

LESSON 13 WORD ACTIVITY MASTER ANSWERS (SEE PAGE 72)
Clues

1. fracture   2. rupture   3. fracture   4. fracture

Synonym Tic-tac-toe

5. ABRUPTLY: (third column) suddenly, unexpectedly, instantly

6. DISRUPT: (diagonal, bottom left to top right) disturb, interrupt, irritate

7. FRAGILITY: (top row) brittleness, delicacy, weakness

8. AMUSEMENT: (diagonal, top left to bottom right) entertainment, recreation, merriment

Sentences

9. Answers will vary but a possible answer follows. *Fragments* are bound to be *fractional* parts because they are pieces from a larger "whole." They are parts, therefore fractions, of something that was once unbroken and complete.

10. Answers will vary.

LESSON 14 WORD ACTIVITY MASTER ANSWERS (SEE PAGE 73)
Matching

| 1. C | 2. E | 3. B | 4. A | 5. D |

Antonyms

| 6. basement | 7. positive | 8. bass | 9. exposed | 10. mixture |

True or False

Ask students to explain their answers and have them debate any differences.

| 11. True | 12. False | 13. True | 14. False | 15. False |

LESSON 15 WORD ACTIVITY MASTER ANSWERS (SEE PAGE 74)
Synonym Tic-tac-toe

1. REFLECT: (second row) think, consider, ponder

2. RELATE: (second column) tell, report, speak

3. COMMITTEE: (diagonal, left top to right bottom) group, council, board

4. COMMUNICATE: (diagonal, left bottom to right top) inform, talk, explain

Other Synonyms

| 5. say, notify | 6. declare, announce | 7. disclose, convey | 8. converse, reveal |

Sentences

9. Answers will vary.   10. Sentences will vary.

WORD LIST

(Numbers in parentheses refer to the lesson in which the word appears.)

abrupt (13)

aquaculture (5)

aquamarine (5)

aquatic   (5)

astronaut (6)

astronomical (6)

astronomy (6)

basement (14)

basis (14)

bass (14)

circuit (1)

circular (1)

circulate (1)

civics (9)

civil (9)

civilian (9)

civility (9)

committee (15)

communicate (15)

composition (14)

conjunction (15)

construction (11)

contraction (11)

converse (15)

coordinate (9)

cycle (1)

cyclone (1)

dependent (2)

destructive (11)

diameter (10)

dispose (14)

disrupt (13)

equality (2)

equate (2)

equator (2)

equidistant (2)

equilateral (2)

exposure (14)

extract (11)

extraordinary (9)

fractional (13)

fracture (13)

fragility (13)

fragment (13)

geometry (10)

inactive (7)

informal (7)

insignificant (7)

insomnia (7)

interactive (3)

interfere (3)

intermittent (3)

interruption (13)

intersect (3)

interval (3)

Mediterranean (5)

metronome (10)

ordinarily (9)

pending (2)

pendulum (2)

perimeter (10)

position (14)

positive (14)

protractor (11)

reaction (15)

reconstruct (11)

recycle (1)

reelect (15)

reflect (15)

relate (15)

retract (11)

rupture (13)

semiannual (7)

semicircle (1)

semicolon (7)

semiconscious (7)

semiformal (7)

semiprecious (7)

structure (11)

subterranean (5)

symmetrical (10)

telecast (6)

teleconference (6)

telegraph (6)

telemarketing (6)

telescope (6)

terrace (5)

terrain (5)

territory (5)

thermal (10)

thermometer (10)

thermostat (10)

traction (11)

transact (3)

transfer (3)

transfusion (3)

transmit (3)

uncivilized (9)

unicycle (1)